Planting for Privacy

Planting for Privacy
A Guide to Growing Hedges and Screens

Judy Horton

Kangaroo Press

With thanks to Chris and Penni

Acknowledgments
I would like to acknowledge the assistance of Michael Gleeson of Castle-Lyn Nursery and Roger Nancarrow of Camellia Magic nursery.

Photographs by Rob and Judy Horton

Cover: The cover photo, by Keva North *(Australian Garden Journal)*, shows the Long Border at Milton Park Country House Hotel, Bowral, NSW. Cover design by Darian Causby.

First published in 1992 by Kangaroo Press Pty Ltd
3 Whitehall Road (P.O. Box 75) Kenthurst NSW 2156
Typeset by G.T. Setters Pty Limited
Printed in Singapore through Global Com Pte Ltd

ISBN 0 86417 472 1

Contents

The Quest For Privacy

The ancient Egyptians were some of the first people to deliberately plant desirable trees and shrubs and, because of Egypt's dry climate, they had to find ways to irrigate their plantations. They found that irrigation was much easier if the plants were arranged in straight rows and this led to an acceptance of formal designs for ancient Egyptian, Greek and Roman gardens. By contrast, early gardens in China and Japan evolved in a more sympathetic climate and thus were more likely to imitate the soft forms of nature.

In ancient Rome, gardens surrounded the homes of the rich and powerful and these leading citizens could reinforce their feelings of power by controlling the surrounding landscape. Trees that could be clipped, shaped and reduced in size were as subservient as the slaves captured by conquering armies. Gardens came to be seen as an extension of architecture and the idea of the 'outdoor room' developed.

Like rooms inside a house, outside rooms need walls to maintain privacy. Rows of fine-foliaged plants can create such walls and also impose formality on the landscape. Thus, the first hedges combined the trend for formality with the desire for privacy. Hedges of clipped plants were also found to give shelter from cold and rain and, if tall enough, to function as a windbreak which protected the outdoor room.

The idea of keeping plants in subjugation was carried from ancient Greece and Rome to western Europe, and formal landscape control reached its peak in the parterre gardens of Versailles in 17th century France. These 'parterres' were laid as patterns of low, clipped hedges that enclosed beds of colourful flowers. In a blending of eastern and western cultures the designs of parterres were often taken from Chinese and Indian embroidery patterns.

By the 18th century, English landowners began to move away from the rigidity of formal gardens, opting instead for a more natural look. This trend influenced the development of gardens in America and, later, in Australia. Instead of whole gardens being dominated by straight lines and clipped, squared-off bushes, such hedges were only placed where they served a definite purpose. The idea of 'working' hedges, that functioned to provide shelter or privacy, was born.

The popularity of hedges increased with the development, in the 19th century, of the middle class, and the growth of suburbs around cities; each house on its own plot of land. Families living on such small pockets of land valued their privacy and hedges were grown to guard that privacy from the neighbours. Low, front hedges were also grown, not so much as a screen, but to demonstrate the dominance and possession of the landowner.

Formal hedges are usually grown from fine-leafed bushes that are regularly clipped and so are labour intensive. That may have been all right for the ancient Romans, who were supplied with slave labour, and for landowners in past eras who had feudal peasants or low paid workers to maintain their estates, but is a little more difficult in these days of high labour costs. This has led to the increased use of low-maintenance, informal hedges and screens.

An informal hedge is made up of a row of plants that are not clipped to shape but are allowed to grow naturally. Whereas a hedge is always made up of the one type of plant, screens are created from a mixture. Screens look far more natural in a garden than formal hedges do, and require much less maintenance, but they seldom have the dramatic effect of a clipped, shaped hedge. They can be made up of a mixture of fast-growing and slow-growing plants, with the speedy growers being culled as the others mature.

Of course, screens can be made from non-living materials and these do have their place in the garden, but they are usually more expensive to create than a living screen and need to be softened by some plant material. Even that most desirable of garden structures — a stone wall — looks more effective if its nooks and crannies are filled with small trailers. Garden walls and fences are often improved by the addition of a climbing plant to soften their outlines.

Even though an informal hedge or screen does not need to be cut into rigid shapes, it will still benefit from light trimming to keep the growth thick and healthy. This is best done by studying the plant's natural shape and shortening the longest stems during the growing period.

Nowadays, the concept of the private garden is more precious than ever. Our cities have expanded and blocks of land have become smaller while the idea of the 'outdoor room' is today more valued than ever. Travelling through built-up areas reveals many sad attempts to establish a living screen that have failed — either through poor plant selection or because of poor maintenance. It is important to put care and thought into the selection of the right plant for the job because a loss in a hedge or screen — whether formal or informal — is a far greater tragedy than an everyday garden demise. A hole in a hedge looks like a tooth that has been knocked out from a perfect smile!

Propagation

When creating a single species screen or, even more importantly, a formal, clipped hedge, it is important that the plants should be as uniform in growth as possible. If buying plants from a nursery, ensure that they are all from the one source and are the same age. If necessary order the plants ahead of time from a propagation nursery. Small plants in tiny pots are called 'tubestock' and substantial numbers can be grown to order.

Buying plants in quantity, even at the smallest size, is expensive and you may like to try your hand at propagating your own. As a general rule, shrubs are propagated vegetatively from cuttings or layers, whereas trees are grown from seed. Seed-grown plants develop the tap root structure that is so important to the stability of trees.

Taking Cuttings

To achieve uniform growth, shrubs are cloned by growing them from cuttings, and for most plants the best time to do this is in the late summer or during autumn. Tip pieces that are taken at this time are called semi-hardwood cuttings and have hardened enough not to wilt, even though they start off with no roots to supply water. If the same cutting was made in spring, the soft new growth would wither before it had time to develop roots.

Most deciduous shrubs can be propagated using hardwood cuttings, which are taken in the winter time when the plant is completely dormant. In the cold part of the year, the plant stores reserves of water in the stem and this helps stop the cuttings from drying out. Hardwood cuttings usually take a longer time to develop roots than semi-hardwood cuttings.

Recent technology has done much to improve the strike rate of cuttings. Modern propagators are able to use glasshouses, misting systems, bottom heat and rooting hormones to help the cuttings form roots as quickly as possible.

Glasshouses allow good light penetration, trap high humidity, and bend the sun's rays so that the heat becomes trapped in the enclosed area. Very few home gardeners are lucky enough to own a glasshouse but they can improvise by using a plastic covered frame or even the clear base of a soft drink bottle.

Misting systems are electronically controlled to spray the cuttings with a fine layer of water at periodic intervals. This helps them get through that critical period when the roots are forming. Of course it is usually impractical for a home gardener to have an electronic misting system but, if the cuttings are covered with clear plastic, a small, moist micro-climate will be created.

Bottom heat is supplied by electric cables that are laid in a bed of coarse sand. The cuttings sit in pots on top of this bed and the gentle heat seems to encourage root formation. Small, electrically controlled home propagating boxes are available (often advertised in garden magazines) and these can be plugged in at home to create bottom heat for cuttings and seed germination. The most sophisticated types even come with a misting facility, but be sure that you will be growing enough cuttings to make your investment worthwhile.

Fortunately, rooting hormones are readily available in nurseries and they do seem to significantly encourage root formation. Sometimes they are marketed for specific cutting types (for example semi-hardwood) but more often they are for general use. They can come in powder form or as a liquid and should be used sparingly. Don't think that if a little bit is good, then more must be better!

Cuttings should be taken from the most recent season's growth. The cutting should contain at least two plant nodes — one to develop the roots and one to form an above ground shoot. Cut just below a node (that's the little mark on the stem where the leaves or shoots come from) and take off all the leaves except the top two. Of course, if it's a hardwood cutting there will be no leaves to worry about! If possible use a very sharp knife to make the cut because even the best secateurs can bruise the plant tissue. If using a hormone treatment, dip the root end into the hormone and shake off the excess.

When you place your cuttings in the pot, make a small hole for each one with a pencil. This means that you won't remove any hormone powder as you push the piece of plant into the mix. You can use any sort of well-drained potting mix but the best results will be achieved if you make a propagating mix using half coarse sand and half peat or perlite. This combination strikes a good balance between water retention and drainage and is suitable for all cuttings.

Gently press the potting mix around the base of the cutting and water well, then provide some sort of cover made out of clear plastic or glass. Wire hoops with their ends pushed into the pot will support a clear plastic bag, or a jar or base of a clear plastic bottle can be upended over the cuttings. This cover should be inside the rim of the pot so that, if necessary, it is easy to apply more water. Make sure you do all this preparation in the shade and keep your cuttings in a cool place out of the sun. You can put a number of cuttings into one pot and carefully separate them after the roots have formed.

Layering

Some shrubs are propagated by layering. This is an ideal method for the home gardener because the success rate is very high, but you need to have large quantities of plant material.

There are two main types of layers: air layers and ground layers. Air layering can be used on most shrubs and involves selecting a piece of the plant (30 cm would be a good length) and making a cut partway through the stem. Put a small amount of damp sphagnum moss into the cut to hold it open and wrap more damp moss right around the cut section. Cover the moss with aluminium wrap so that the whole thing is as airtight as possible. After a few weeks you can partially unwrap the aluminium foil to see if any roots have formed, but you will need some patience as root growth can be a slow process. Keep the sphagnum moss well covered until plenty of roots are visible and then sever the new plant from its parent and pot it up. This is an easy way of propagating camellias.

For ground layering, choose a branch that can be pulled down to the ground, make a similar cut on the underside of the branch, and bury the cut in the soil. It is important to fix the branch securely so that the cut section will not be uncovered. Hoops made out of lengths of wire are cheap and easy to push into the ground and will hold the branch firmly in place. Azaleas can be propagated in this manner and low parts of the plant will often form natural layers.

Growing Seeds

Most trees are grown from seed and it is important to make sure that all the seed for one variety comes from a single source. Some special tree cultivars must be grafted onto a seedling rootstock but this is a bit beyond the scope of the average home gardener.

Most seeds come encased in some sort of fruit or pod which should be removed before the seed is sown. Collect the fruit when it is ripe and soak it in water to remove any soft flesh. If the seeds are wrapped in a pod or capsule, place the ripe capsule inside a paper bag and leave it to open by itself. This way, you will be able to capture the seeds in a clean, dry atmosphere.

Some seeds need special treatment before sowing. The classic example is the *Acacia* genus (wattles) whose seeds must have boiling water poured over them before they will germinate. It seems that they need to be fooled into thinking that a bushfire has passed through the area.

Spring is the best time to sow seeds, although most can be started during early summer if they are well looked after on hot days. Place a loose layer of commercial seed raising mix in a flat tray and softly press the seeds into the surface. Cover them lightly and water gently so they are not disturbed.

Keep the tray in a shady area and don't let it dry out. As soon as the seedlings are large enough to handle they can be potted on into small individual pots. Native plants grow particularly quickly and can usually be planted out in the garden during the first growing season.

Division

Dividing plants is often the simplest and easiest way of acquiring new ones, but it can also be a slow process because it is limited by the plant's rate of growth. Division is only used on those plants that spread by clumping or by sending out some kind of underground shoot. Most of the strappy-leaved plants such as agapanthus, mondo grass and cliveas, as well as deciduous clumpers like may bushes, can be divided into two or more plants.

Division is merely the physical act of breaking the plant into parts with some roots attached. It can be done with a sharp spade or even by using your favourite carving knife. It is best done in the plant's dormant period in late winter, just before the new growth starts.

Planting and Maintenance

Preparing the Soil

The first step to take when planting a new hedge or screen is to clear the planting area of grass. Mark out a strip bed at least a metre wide and remove the grass by digging or poisoning with herbicide. The safest herbicide to use is glyphosate, which breaks down very quickly once it contacts the soil. Glyphosate is most commonly sold as Zero® or Roundup®. Read the instructions carefully as the mixing rate will vary according to which product is used and the type of grass you are dealing with. Although they are based on the same chemical, Roundup is usually more than three times stronger than Zero, and you will find that couch grass is much harder to kill than kikuyu.

If you have used glyphosate and you are confident, after a few weeks, that the grass has been completely destroyed, you can dig the dead grass into the soil where it will become additional organic matter. Don't do this, however, if there are any seed heads present because they will germinate and start the whole process again. It is important that the planting area be cleared because grass roots can compete with the plant's feeding roots and significantly slow its growth rate.

If your soil is sandy, its capacity to hold water and nutrients can be increased by adding old compost, manure or leaves. With clay soil, its ability to 'breathe' and let water move through quickly will be enhanced by the incorporation of — you guessed it — old compost, manure or leaves! So, whatever your soil type, start by digging in a generous layer of any organic matter that you can get hold of. Don't skimp on this aspect of the preparation; it's unlikely that you will have enough home-made compost and it will be worth paying for a load of milled cow manure or mushroom compost.

Clay soil can also be made more functional by digging gypsum or liquid clay-breaker into the planting area. These chemicals change the structure of the soil so that it is more open to air and water movement.

Don't despair if you have a clay soil — after you improve the structure of such soil it makes a very good base on which to establish a garden.

Fertilising

Australian soils are poor in nutrients and most introduced plants will need plenty of supplementary fertilising to compensate for this deficiency. At planting time some bands of fertiliser can be dug in along the sides of the planting area. The idea is that the roots will be able to grow out to the fertiliser; they should not be in direct contact with the fertiliser at planting time. This is especially important if dry, chemical fertilisers are used because they are the most likely to burn young roots.

Using fertiliser is an ongoing commitment. It is even more important when the plant is established than when it is young, and this is the time when most people tend to take their garden plants for granted. Just because they've been there for a long time, don't assume that the plants' needs are being met. Indeed, it is likely that an old plant will have used up all the goodness in the growing area so it is even more desirable to fertilise on a regular basis. Try to use a complete fertiliser at least once a year, preferably in spring, and follow up by renewing the layer of organic mulch over the root system. Even native plants will benefit from an annual boost but make sure that you use a fertiliser that has been formulated for Australian plants. Fertiliser should always be applied to damp soil and should be well watered in.

Planting

Planting is best done in spring or autumn, although some deciduous trees and shrubs are more readily available in winter and should be planted out then. Plants for hedges and screens are usually spaced much more closely than they would be in a normal garden situation. The general rule for a formal, clipped hedge is that the plants should be placed at one quarter of the plant's ultimate width. Because of these competitive conditions, soil preparation and plant maintenance is all important.

When planting, dig a hole that is about the same depth as the pot but at least twice its width. Make sure that the sides of the hole are not too smooth, as any hard surface will be difficult for roots to penetrate. If you must use a post-hole digger, break up the sides of the planting hole so that roots will be encouraged to move outwards. In a farm situation it is probably better to dig an open planting trench using a tractor.

Gently remove the plant from the pot, keeping the potting mix intact so that root disturbance is minimal. Place the plant in the hole, making sure that the top surface of the potting mix is no lower than the surrounding ground level. Use some of the soil that has been dug out of the hole to fill any gaps around the base of the plant and then water well — preferably with a fixed sprinkler. This will eliminate air pockets and firm the soil around the roots. It's not necessary to 'stamp' the soil into place because such heavy-booted activity could break many of the roots. After watering, place a layer of mulch over the root system.

Watering

The plant's growth rate will largely depend on whether it is given a satisfactory supply of water. Remember that Australia receives less rainfall than most other parts of the world, so if you have selected plants from moister climates they are going to need some help. This is even more important with a hedge or screen because it is so closely planted and the plants are growing in competition with each other.

There are many modern aids to watering and some of the most efficient are the watering systems that have an outlet at each plant. These are available as do-it-yourself kits or can be installed by an expert. They can even be controlled by an automatic timer that will, unlike even the best of gardeners, always remember to turn on the tap.

In home garden situations, the simplest type of watering system will direct a little spray of water at the base of each plant but in very dry areas, or in districts with doubtful water quality, drippers are used which drop water right above the plant's roots. The slow percolation of the water through the soil removes most of the salt and accumulated minerals. Many of these drip methods were developed by the Israelis to overcome their twin problems of dry climate and salty water, and are ideal for the drier parts of Australia.

An even simpler type of water system is the soaker hose, which has a series of fine holes along its length. These holes seep water onto the root system and wastage is minimal. Ideally, one soaker hose should be placed on either side of the row of plants to ensure even distribution of the water.

Water-holding gels are able to hold hundreds of times their own weight in water and can be mixed with the soil in the planting hole before planting. The granules store water until it is extracted by the roots of the plant. This substantially reduces the amount of supplementary watering required and may mean that the plant can happily survive from one rainfall to the next.

Periodic and thorough soakings are always preferable to short, frequent bursts of water. Short waterings only manage to wet the surface of the soil and encourage the roots to stay near the top, whereas longer soakings train roots to grow down to the reserve of moisture at the deeper level. Water that is applied in the evening lasts longer in the soil than any that is sprinkled in the heat of the day. Watering by hand is better than no watering, but a hand-held hose is seldom left in one place long enough for the water to thoroughly penetrate to the depths (it's amazing — you feel as if you have been standing in one spot for an hour with the hose, but sometimes it's been less than a minute!).

The greatest aid to retaining moisture in the soil is a thick layer of organic mulch over the surface. If this is renewed annually it adds humus and nutrients to the soil, aids in water penetration, retains moisture, prevents weed growth and evens out temperature fluctuations.

Pruning and Clipping

The most important rule to follow when pruning hedges and screens is to start cutting long before the plant has approached the desired height. This means that the plant makes thick growth with lots of small branches and short intervals between these branches. Don't wait until your hedge reaches the size you want before you start cutting because you will end up with lots of sticks and no leaves on the top.

Hedges should always be shaped so that the base is slightly wider than the top. This helps the hedge to remain stable and ensures that sunlight can reach right down to the base (this is especially important for conifers). When clipping a formal hedge, only the most experienced are able to rely on their own eyes to guide them. I need a string line to keep my hedge straight and you will probably find that you do too.

Fine, close growth should be sheared with hedge shears. These are the classic, long-bladed tools that the Victorian head gardeners wielded with such dexterity and they have changed little since those days. Unfortunately, garden staffing arrangements have, and you are most likely to find that a clipped, formal hedge is very much a 'do-it-yourself' project. You may be glad, in that case, to use a pair of the electrically-operated shears that are available. They probably don't cut quite as finely as the hand tools but when the job is done so much more quickly and easily, who's quibbling!

For a sheared hedge, you will need to grow plants with fine, small leaves. Plants with larger leaves should have their stems clipped, between the leaf nodes, using secateurs. When large leaves are cut with shears, the resulting effect is ragged and untidy. Buy the best secateurs or shears that you can afford and keep them dry, well-oiled and sharpened. Any branches bigger than finger thickness should be lopped, using long-handled loppers, or sawn with a pruning saw.

The best plants to choose for a clipped hedge are those that will grow a little bigger than the finished height you desire. This means that you are not setting yourself an impossible maintenance task, but gives you enough leeway to be able to trim the top to a thick and bushy finish.

It is impossible to give a fixed regime for clipping. Most formally hedged plants will need to be cut two or three times in a growing season but, for a less formal look, a trimming just after flowering may be all that is needed. The best idea is to watch the growth and trim when you think it's necessary.

Hedges For Edges

Dwarf hedges are used as a decoration in a garden or to define a garden bed or a particular part of a landscape. They are generally kept low so that they don't interfere with the view of the area they are outlining. Edge gardens have their origins in the knot or parterre gardens of more formal times.

One of the most popular forms of edging is to use a row of annuals. This can be an attractive and economical short-term solution, but permanent plantings give a long-term sculptural shape to the garden.

Traditionally, box species have been used for edging and, because of their close foliage, they react very well to clipping. A friend of Julius Caesar is supposed to have been the first person to cut box to shape, and it is still popularly used for topiary. *Buxus sempervirens* 'Suffruticosa', a dwarf form of the hedging box, is commonly called 'edging box' because it has been employed so often for this purpose. Unfortunately, it is slow growing and very expensive to buy in quantity — and it really should be bought in quantity because a skimpy box hedge is worse than no hedge at all. When planting, small plants in 200-millimetre pots should be placed so that if they were to be left in the containers, the sides of the pots would touch each other. This means that the plant centres would be 200 millimetres apart. Certainly, never plant more than 300 millimetres apart.

All *Buxus* species grow from tip cuttings that can be taken in late summer and autumn, but rooted cuttings of dwarf edging box are best grown on in a pot for at least two seasons before planting out.

There is another dwarf cultivar, *B. microphylla* var. *microphylla*, that seems to grow a little faster and may consequently be cheaper to purchase.

Dwarf box hedges can be kept as low as 15 centimetres in height although if uncut, they will ultimately grow to one metre.

Box plants suit all but tropical climates and will grow in sun or part shade. They have green, glossy leaves but very insignificant flowers.

Box honeysuckle, *Lonicera nitida*, is often grown as a substitute for box because it is faster growing and, consequently, cheaper to buy. It is quite unlike most of the other honeysuckles and has tiny, close foliage that reacts well to clipping with shears. The cultivar 'Aurea' has bright yellow new leaves in spring that age to an old-gold colour in summer. If left uncut, box honeysuckle will grow to two metres but can be clipped to less than 30 centimetres. Clipping should be commenced when the plants are very young as this will encourage close, dense growth. It grows easily from cuttings that should be taken in late summer or autumn.

Box honeysuckle is happy in most climates but can become thin in periods of humidity.

Another small plant that handles most climates is a dwarf form of the Japanese spindle-tree (*Euonymus japonicus* 'Silver Pillar'). This plant has pale green leaves that are edged with creamy-white and has very close growth that is similar to the dwarf box. Like the dwarf box, it should be planted at 200-millimetre centres and grows very slowly. It needs a well drained position in full sun.

Some dwarf conifers can be used as low edges but many varieties are hard to buy because their slow growth makes them unpopular with nurserymen. They are best confined to cold climates and are much easier to obtain in nurseries in such areas. Look for some of the false cypress (*Chamaecyparis*) cultivars, such as *C. obtusa* 'Nana-aurea'. Some can be kept as low as 30 centimetres. In warmer districts, use the rheingold thuja (*Thuja occidentalis* 'Rheingold') which grows in a wide climatic range. I don't think it's worth even attempting conifers in a tropical or subtropical climate. You might get away with an isolated specimen, but planting a row would be tempting fate.

Other low shrubs that are suitable for clipped borders are the Tom Thumb pittosporum and *Serissa foetida*, which is most commonly seen in its cultivar 'Snowleaves'. *Pittosporum* 'Tom Thumb' is a dwarf form of the purple-leafed New Zealand pittosporum, and has a compact growth habit and very dark purplish-black leaves. It can be clipped to about 30 centimetres. It will grow in semi-shade but needs full sun to bring out the best dark colour in its leaves.

Like the pittosporum, *S. foetida* 'Snowleaves' grows in a wide range of climates but needs plenty of sun to keep a good foliage cover. It is called 'Snowleaves' because of the white edges on the leaves. If clipped from an early stage it develops dense growth, hiding the small white flowers that grow in the leaf axils. It is often grown as a quick bonsai so may be available as a bonsai 'starter' from specialist nurseries.

In suitable climates some of the dwarf lavenders can be used as an edging, but they are really best in a dry area as they tend to be shortlived in warm, humid districts. Look for lavender that is labelled 'Dwarf' or 'Munstead' and plant in a well-drained, sunny position. The grey foliage makes an interesting colour contrast. A similar effect can be achieved when you use cotton lavender (*Santolina chamaecyparissus*) which likes to grow in the same conditions as the true lavenders but produces bright yellow summer flowers. Light clipping after flowering will keep the bush from becoming leggy.

An almost trouble-free plant that also makes a good colour contrast is the dwarf nandina (*Nandina domestica* 'Pygmaea'). This grows to about half a metre and produces a clump of vertical, slender, bamboo-like stems that are clad in dull green leaves. The leaves really come into their own in winter, however, when the cold brings out a strong red pigmentation. Nandina will withstand temperatures down to – 10°C and the colder the weather, the better the colour but even in subtropical areas it will put on a creditable show of colour. The leaves stay green all year round if the plant is in a shady spot.

It is most important that the plants chosen for a border should be reliable and suitable for the climate and position. This means that you sometimes feel that you see the same plants everywhere, but it is better to have an edge that is slightly boring than one that is only half alive. The border plant that is most often labelled as 'boring' is the lily of the Nile (*Agapanthus orientalis*). This would be worth growing just for the effect of its strappy leaves, but it goes on to produce a leafless flower stem in summer that can be up to a metre tall and is crowned by a ball of tubular blue or white bells. Agapanthus is used extensively because it is almost totally reliable. As long as it has good drainage, it can grow in most positions in climates ranging from the tropics to moderately frosty areas. It flowers best in a sunny spot but will happily survive in heavy shade.

The foliage clumps of agapanthus grow up to half a metre but there are now some dwarf forms available that stay at half that, or even less. There is great variation in the size of so-called dwarf agapanthus, so it is always best to buy your plants all at once and from the one supplier. The same could be said of full-sized agapanthus, because there are some different species and cultivars available, and the naming of the various types is quite unreliable.

Like agapanthus, the African iris (*Dietes* species), as their common name suggests, come from Africa and so suit the Australian climate.

They are extraordinarily tough and drought resistant. *D. bicolor* has pale yellow flowers that are marked with a darker blotch, while *D. grandiflora* has larger white blooms with lavender and yellow patches. Both flower over a long period in the warmer months but should have their flower heads removed before the seeds develop because the plants have been known to spread to bushland. African iris grow to about the same size as agapanthus and are reliable border plants.

Other strap-leafed plants make excellent borders and will provide a foliage contrast in a garden bed. Ribbon grass (*Liriope muscari*) is usually grown in its variegated form with cream stripes on the edges of the dark green, grass-like foliage. 'Muscari' in the botanic name refers to the similarity of the purple flower spikes to those of the grape hyacinth, *Muscari botryoides*. Ribbon grass will grow in a wide range of climates but must have an open, well-drained position.

Daylilies (*Hemerocallis* hybrids) are becoming increasingly popular and American and Australian hybridisers have worked hard in recent years to produce plants with better blooms and smaller growth. Daylilies grow in a wide climatic range, but some varieties die down completely in winter and are best used as garden specimens rather than in a border.

Daylily clumps vary enormously in height and, before selecting mixed colours for a border, you should consult one of the specialist nurseries that take mail orders from all over Australia. Their tempting catalogues contain full descriptions of height, colour and the special characteristics of each variety. Each flower only lasts for one day — which is why they are called daylilies — but you can have a succession of flowering for months. The clumps of mid-green foliage look good along the edge of a path or driveway.

Daylilies will tolerate dry conditions but look at their best in quite damp soil. The same conditions suit the Australian native mat rush, *Lomandra longifolia*. This plant forms a large tussock of glossy, strap-like leaves with curiously chewed-looking ends. It will grow in sun or shade to about 70 centimetres. The cream flower spikes, which are more obvious on female plants, are shorter than the leaves but attract attention in warm weather because of their strong, banana-like perfume. Mat rush can be used to edge a driveway or a bed of tall growing native shrubs. Kangaroo paws will create a similar effect but I don't think that they are reliable enough for a border.

A very low border plant that could be used more often may be overlooked because it always comes last in alphabetical plant listings. With a botanical name like *Zephyranthes candida* it's no wonder that people steer clear, but if you use the common name, storm lily, gardeners are much happier. These plants have year-round clumps of shiny, grass-like leaves but look stunning after periods of heavy rain — hence the name 'storm lily' — when they burst forth with stems topped with white, crocus-like blooms.

The current trend in strappy edging plants is to use the Japanese mondo grass (*Ophiopogon japonicus*). It will grow in sun or shade but tends to look a bit tired in a sunny spot and I prefer to see the dark, sombre green in a cool, sheltered part of the garden. As a border to a shady bed, mondo grass is hard to beat and its narrow leaves droop over a path in a most engaging manner. It will produce spikes of small white flowers and blue berries in summer, but these are mostly hidden in the foliage.

Another popular choice for borders in shaded gardens is the kaffir lily (*Clivea miniata*) which burns quite badly if exposed to summer sun. Kaffir lily looks good under established trees and its fleshy surface roots can survive in competitive situations. It sends up a leafless flower stalk in late winter that is topped with bell-shaped, bright orange-scarlet blooms. It grows to about half a metre tall but will only survive in a frost-free climate. It is grown from division, which means that it is sometimes hard to buy. Another variety, *C. nobilis*, has narrower, darker flowers and can be even harder to get hold of.

Checklist: Hedges For Edges

Agapanthus orientalis (**Lily of the Nile**)
Height: 50 cm.
Minimum Spacing: 30 cm.
Propagation: Division.
Comments: Flower spikes can reach one metre in height. Some dwarf varieties available. Strap leaves.

Buxus microphylla **var.** *microphylla* (**Dwarf Edging Box**)
Height: 1 m.
Cut to: 15 cm minimum. All year.
Minimum Spacing: 20 cm.
Propagation: Semi-hardwood cuttings.
Comments: Slow growing.

B. sempervirens 'Suffruticosa' (Dwarf Edging Box)
Height: 90 cm.
Cut to: 15 cm minimum. All year.
Minimum Spacing: 20 cm.
Propagation: Semi-hardwood cuttings.
Comments: Very slow growing.

Chamaecyparis obtusa 'Nana-aurea' (Dwarf False Cypress)
Height: 1.2m.
Cut to: 30 cm.
Minimum Spacing: 30 cm.
Propagation: Semi-hardwood cuttings.
Comments: Very slow growing.

Clivea miniata, C. nobilis (Kaffir Lily)
Height: 50 cm.
Minimum Spacing: 30 cm.
Propagation: Division.
Comments: For frost-free shade. Strap leaves.

Dietes bicolor, D. grandiflora (African Iris)
Height: 50 cm.
Minimum Spacing: 30 cm.
Propagation: Division.
Comments: Hardy and drought resistant. Strap leaves.

Euonymus japonicus 'Silver Pillar' (Japanese Spindle Tree)
Height: 50 cm.
Cut to: 30 cm. All year.
Minimum Spacing: 20 cm.
Propagation: Semi-hardwood cuttings.
Comments: Very slow growing.

Hemerocallis hybrids (Daylily)
Height: Varies to 1 m.
Minimum Spacing: 50 cm.
Propagation: Division.
Comments: Some varieties die down in winter. Strap leaves.

Lavandula angustifolia 'Munstead' (Dwarf Lavender)
Height: 30 cm.
Cut to: 20 cm. After flowering.

Minimum Spacing: 20 cm.
Propagation: Tip cuttings all year.

Liriope muscari (Ribbon Grass)
Height: 30 cm.
Minimum Spacing: 20 cm.
Propagation: Division.
Comments: Strap leaves.

Lomandra longifolia (Mat Rush)
Height: 70 cm.
Minimum Spacing: 30 cm.
Propagation: Division, seed.
Comments: Very hardy. Strap leaves.

Lonicera nitida (Box Honeysuckle)
Height: 2 m.
Cut to: 30 cm.
Minimum Spacing: 30 cm.
Propagation: Semi-hardwood cuttings.
Comments: Needs good drainage.

Nandina domestica 'Pygmaea' (Dwarf Nandina)
Height: 50 cm.
Cut to: 30 cm. Late winter.
Minimum Spacing: 20 cm.
Propagation: Division.
Comments: Leaves turn red in winter sun.

Ophiopogon japonicus (Mondo Grass)
Height: 25 cm.
Minimum Spacing: 10 cm.
Propagation: Division.
Comments: Strap leaves.

Pittosporum tenuifolium 'Tom Thumb' (Tom Thumb Pittosporum)
Height: 75 cm.
Cut to: 30 cm. Late winter.
Minimum Spacing: 20 cm.
Propagation: Semi-hardwood cuttings.
Comments: Needs sun for good colour.

Santolina chamaecyparissus (**Cotton Lavender**)
Height: 50 cm.
Cut to: 40 cm. Clip lightly after flowering.
Minimum Spacing: 30 cm.
Propagation: Semi-hardwood cuttings in late summer.
Comments: Needs good sun and well drained soil.

Serissa foetida '**Snowleaves**' (**Snowleaves**)
Height: 60 cm.
Cut to: 40 cm. Spring, summer, autumn.
Minimum Spacing: 20 cm.
Propagation: Semi-hardwood cuttings.
Comments: Dense, twiggy growth.

Thuja occidentalis '**Rheingold**' (**Rheingold Thuja**)
Height: 1 m.
Cut to: 50 cm. Early spring.
Minimum Spacing: 30 cm.
Propagation: Semi-hardwood cuttings. Also ground layers.
Comments: Cut off any upright shoots. This thuja turns an old gold colour in winter.

Zephyranthes candida (**Storm Lily**)
Height: 20 cm.
Minimum Spacing: 20 cm.
Propagation: Division or seed.
Comments: Grass-like leaves. White flowers after periods of heavy rain.

Low Hedges and Screens (1 to 1.5 m)

Hedges of this height are seen primarily as decorations and as markers for dividing areas because they are not really tall enough to make a visual barrier. It is a bonus, therefore, if the plants used have attractive leaves or flowers, or present a pleasing foliage contrast. Remember that a hedge that is constantly clipped will not flower as well as one that is left to grow naturally so, if flowering is important, select a plant that will grow to the height you want without being trimmed.

You can choose to make a formal hedge using a row of one plant that is clipped to shape, or an informal screen that is made up of mixed plantings. When choosing plant material for low hedges, try to select shrubs with relatively small leaves which will look in proportion with the height of the hedge.

Flowering Hedges and Screens

The glossy abelia (*Abelia* x *grandiflora*) is one of the most versatile of plants. As long as it has a reasonable amount of sunshine, glossy abelia keeps its good looks all year round. In the summer it produces waves of small, white bells that are followed by a showy pink calyx. Abelia seems to suit all climates and is evergreen, although the leaves turn a red shade in winter in frosty areas. There is also a form with golden leaves that makes a good colour contrast.

Escallonias grow in a similar manner with arching canes coming from near the base of the shrub. The most commonly seen is the red-flowered escallonia (*Escallonia rubra* var. *macrantha*), which has bunches of red-pink bell flowers, but there are other varieties with blooms in shades ranging from white through all stages of pink. Escallonia comes from the colder parts of Chile and seems willing to accept a wide range of climates, although it is only hardy down to about − 5°C.

Another 'toughie' is the Indian hawthorn (*Raphiolepis indica*) which grows slowly to about three metres but is easily kept clipped at less than half that. In areas near the coast it has a tendency to seed into bushland, so it is wise to cut off the bunches of white flowers before the blue-black berries form. The Japanese hawthorn, *R. umbellata*, which resents being clipped, has similar white blooms but the hybrid of the Indian and Japanese hawthorns, *R.* × *delacourii*, has pretty pink blooms and is even slower growing than its parents.

Hebe, diosma and the Mexican orange blossom all grow in a mixture of climates and make good hedges to about one metre. Hebes are New Zealand shrubs that flower in a range of colours from white to purple and pink. One of the most attractive is *Hebe speciosa* 'La Seduisante' with dark, purplish-red young leaves and spikes of violet flowers. Diosmas (*Coleonema pulchrum*) are from South Africa and need good drainage to flourish. The best type is called 'Nanum' and is a compact grower which is covered with starry, pink blooms for a long time in winter and spring. Mexican orange blossom (*Choisya ternata*) has sprays of white, perfumed flowers in spring. All three do best in an area with low humidity and are relatively cold tolerant. They could be attractively combined to make a one metre high, mixed screen.

Some of the best shrubs for low hedges are the small types of sasanqua camellias. Sasanquas seem to have two distinct growth habits — either tall, stiff and upright or low growing with sideways shoots that are very flexible. The low growing cultivars develop very slowly and are easy to keep to one metre or even less. Low varieties that are most readily available are the pinks, 'Shishi-gashira' and 'Showa-no-sakae', and the white, 'Mine-no-yuki'. 'Yuletide' is a small grower with slow, upright growth and bright red, single flowers that light up shady garden corners.

One of the great virtues of sasanqua camellias is that they will grow almost anywhere. They seem unfussy about climate and happy in either sun or part shade, which makes them ideal for those situations where a hedge moves from a sunny spot into a more sheltered position. Other plants that show such adaptability are the evergreen viburnum (*Viburnum tinus*) and the large, single azaleas.

V. tinus has the complicated common name of laurustinus but is a very simple and attractive plant with dark green leaves and round bunches of small white flowers in winter. It is easily kept to about one metre high or if allowed to grow to its full height will eventually reach three metres. It will survive in all sorts of difficult sites but, naturally, looks best if given good care and watering. There is a variegated form available which has year-round foliage interest but must be grown in at least half sun or its leaves will revert to plain green. Laurustinus leaves are irresistible to thrips so keep a watch out for the tell-tale whitening of the leaf surfaces and the blobs of black excrement on the undersides. Sometimes the problem can be solved by spraying the foliage with water — thrips hate to get caught out in the rain — but you may need to resort to using an insecticide.

The tall, single azaleas make an excellent, although slow growing, hedge to about 1.2 metres. Azaleas are really shade lovers but these tall singles are so hardy that they will grow in full sun in most coastal districts, although they would probably find inland summer sun difficult to withstand. They need acid soil, a generous layer of mulch over the shallow root system and sun for at least a quarter of the day. Temperatures below – 3°C could cause damage to the leaves and flower buds.

Readily available varieties include 'Splendens' (salmon-pink), 'Magnifica' (purple), 'Alba Magna' or 'Mortii' (white), 'Alphonse Anderson' (light and dark pink) and 'Mauve Schryderi' (pale mauve). A mixture of these would give a wonderful colour display. Unlike some of the more recently developed hybrid azaleas, these tend to flower for just a few weeks in spring but the density of the flowering is magnificent.

Azaleas are troubled by two main problems: lace bug and petal blight. Lace bug is a sucking insect pest whose numbers build up over summer and cause the leaves to become pale and silvery. Sometimes the insects can be dislodged by a strong jet of water but it is usually necessary to resort to spraying with a penetrant insecticide such as dimethoate. Petal blight is a fungal disease that makes the flowers collapse just as they are at their peak. It can be controlled by picking off the affected blooms and spraying with a suitable fungicide.

Most other hedging plants have more specific requirements for sun or shade. One sun lover is plumbago, which is enjoying a revival of popularity at the moment. I am not sure how long this period in demand will last because plumbago does need to be clipped frequently in order to keep it tidy. It is often seen as a tangled mess creeping through neglected gardens and this, no doubt, has led to its fall from favour. Only in recent years have gardeners again come to appreciate its profuse flowering and ease of growth. Plumbago can develop to hedge size in one growing season so is ideal if you want a quick cover. The blooms appear all through the warm weather. The blue variety seems to reflect the colour of the summer sky while white plumbago is useful to give a soft, cottage-garden effect. Plumbago will only take very light frosts.

In similar climates, you could hedge with the goldfussia and if you think that common name is a mouthful, try the botanic one, *Strobilanthes anisophyllus*. In spite of this, it is a very pretty plant with mauve bell flowers in spring — and occasionally throughout the year — that contrast well with the purplish-green leaves. Tip pruning during the growing season will make the bush nice and thick, but if you live in a slightly frosty area you will find that the frost will do the nipping back for you. Goldfussia plants have upright growth so, for a hedge, should be planted no more than 60 centimetres from each other.

Goldfussia will not tolerate any but the lightest frosts and neither will the quaintly named yesterday, today and tomorrow (*Brunfelsia bonodora*) whose flowers change colour from dark blue to light blue and then white. It has soft, mid-green leaves and can be kept as a bushy screen to about 1.2 metres. It should be lightly pruned after flowering and occasionally through the growing season. There is a smaller growing form with less attractive foliage but similar flowers called *B. calycina*. Yesterday, today and tomorrow is most suited to a position in morning sun.

One for strictly frost-free areas is the dwarf tibouchina (*Tibouchina* 'Jules') which reaches one metre and turns itself into a ball of bright purple when it flowers in late summer and autumn. I've seen a row of it used in a subtropical district in place of a front fence and the effect is stunning. If you want something a little taller, then use the closely related pink lasiandra (*Melastoma malabathricum*), with mauve-pink blooms at the same time of year.

Don't despair if you garden in a cold district, however, because here you can hedge with the Californian lilac (*Ceanothus* × *veitchianus*) which is usually sold under the variety name 'Blue Pacific'. These plants resent humidity and poor drainage but flourish in an inland region. The flower spikes are an incredibly deep blue and the foliage is shiny and crimped. Clipping to form a hedge will benefit the plant and stop it from becoming leggy.

In cold areas, your choice of hedging plants is wider if you include some of the deciduous flowering shrubs that do so well in cool climates. White may (*Spiraea cantoniensis* 'Lanceata') is often seen as a fence plant where it has room to let its arching branches fall sideways. It flowers profusely in spring and should be pruned hard after flowering. Some of the older canes can be removed completely at pruning time and this will encourage fresh, new growth.

The ornamental quince, or japonica (*Chaenomeles speciosa*), blooms beautifully on bare branches in late winter and spring and makes an effective barrier because it is armed with thorns. It has a number of named cultivars in shades of white, pink and red. One of the most popular is 'Apple Blossom' with pale pink and white, cup-shaped blooms. One way of keeping japonica trimmed is to cut some of the flower sprays for floral arrangements. They are useful for producing a Japanese effect in a vase. Japonica can be grown in warmer climates but, in such areas, it tends to be only partially deciduous and loses much of the striking contrast produced by blossoms sitting on bare branches.

Holly varieties (*Ilex* species) are best in cool climates and, like the japonica, can be used to make a deterrent hedge although, in this case, the spines are on the leaves rather than the branches. Hollies are grown not so much for their flower display as for their decorative fruits. This berrying can be rather a haphazard affair because the plants carry either male or female flowers and only the females go on to produce berries.

Most hollies grow to three metres or more and need to be clipped from an early stage to form a low hedge but there is a dwarf form of the Chinese holly (*I. cornuta*) that only grows to one metre so can be left unclipped to develop at its own pace — which is a slow one!

Foliage Hedges and Screens

Because constant cutting reduces the ability of plants to produce flowers, some of the most successful hedges are made from foliage plants. Plants used in such instances either have insignificant blooms or blooms that are removed in the process of clipping. They are chosen because their foliage has interesting colour or form.

Box plants are the classic hedging plants. They respond beautifully to clipping by producing close, new growth that gives solidity of form to a hedge. *Buxus sempervirens* was originally brought from the Mediterranean countries to western Europe and has become so synonymous with English landscape design that it is commonly called English box. English box has dark green leaves and dense, twiggy growth.

Japanese box (*B. microphylla* var. *japonica*) is similar but has leaves that are more rounded and lighter in colour. These leaves have the curious habit of acquiring some orange pigmentation in the colder months and then changing back to a light, bright green in spring.

Both box plants are most commonly seen as part of formal clipped hedges between 1 and 1.5 metres high. They have insignificant green flowers in spring that herald their presence by releasing a sweet perfume. Box will grow in a wide range of climates but the Japanese type seems to be more tolerant of warm and humid weather.

Another classic hedging plant is *Euonymus japonicus*, the Japanese spindle bush, which is very given to producing colour variegations in its leaves. This means that there is a bewildering array of different leaf types, some of which are superior to others. They mostly have yellow or cream markings in the green of the leaf colour. Japanese spindle bush is evergreen and is excellent if clipped to shape. It was very fashionable for hedges in earlier times and is not used as much nowadays, which is a pity as it seems to be almost indestructible. Like the box, Japanese spindle bush has insignificant flowers.

Another Japanese plant, Japanese oleaster (*Elaeagnus pungens* 'Aurea') has similar variegated leaves and appears to be as tough as the spindle bush. Its leaves have a very hard surface and this helps the plant stand up to exposed, windy positions. Japanese oleaster is often difficult to find in nurseries and you may need to propagate your own plants. This has to be done with semi-hardwood cuttings in autumn as the plant rarely fruits in our climate.

Photinias are most often used for large screens where their clusters of white flowers and bright red new leaves are seen on a grand scale but one variety, *Photinia glabra* 'Rubens', is suitable for a low, sheared hedge if cut two or three times a year. This constant cutting means that the plant very rarely flowers but instead has flushes of shiny, red, new growth in spring and autumn. Other photinias have larger leaves and so are less appropriate as a sheared hedge. Photinias will grow happily in a wide temperature range.

In subtropical and tropical regions, attractive foliage hedges are formed with the Fijian fire plant (*Acalypha wilkesiana*). This shrub is no use at all in cold positions but is very successful in a sheltered, frost-free spot with plenty of summer water. There are many different cultivars available with leaf colours ranging from copper and red, through to variegated cream and green. They should be cut back hard in early spring and fertilised to encourage new growth.

In cold areas a maroon-coloured barrier hedge can be made using

Daylilies (*Hemerocallis* spp.) will make a colourful border.

Clumps of *Dietes bicolor* give an informal look.

Mondo grass edges a shady path.

Hebe grown as a low hedge.

the deciduous purple barberry (*Berberis thunbergii* 'Atropurpurea'). This plant is armed with deterrent spines which will help keep dogs out of the area. One heavy pruning in late winter is often enough to keep the hedge under control for the growing season.

Good use can be made of another foliage shrub, the gold dust plant (*Aucuba japonica* 'Variegata'), in shady parts of the garden because this is one plant that hates to be exposed to strong sunlight. Be careful not to place it in a constantly damp spot, however, because poor drainage causes black spots to develop on the leaves. In its variegated form the dark green leaves are marked with a warm, clear yellow which helps the plant to brighten a shady part of the garden. In a happy position it will grow to two or three metres, but can be clipped to about half that size. It will grow in most climates.

The most adaptable plant for a low hedge is the Japanese sacred bamboo (*Nandina domestica*). This common name often frightens people because they have visions of an invader that will charge through a garden in the same manner as bamboo, but fortunately, this is not the case. Although sacred bamboo does have bamboo-like canes and spreads by means of suckering growth from the base, this increase is a slow affair and very easy to control. Nandina will grow in a wide climatic range in sun or shade and is particularly useful for a low screen in a narrow corridor. The foliage is light and airy so the plant would only form a complete visual block if planted densely in a bed that was more than a metre wide.

Sacred bamboo could be classed as a flowering hedge because it will produce small white flowers in summer and autumn. These can be followed by decorative, red berries which persist well into winter. However it is included as a foliage shrub because it is grown for its handsome leaf effect, rather than its floral display. The soft green leaves can take on a red colouration in the colder months but this will only happen in a sunny aspect. Sacred bamboo can be grown from seed or from division of the clumps in late winter.

Natives

Many native shrubs have evolved to grow quickly when conditions are favourable and to rapidly reach reproductive stage so that the continuation of the species can be assured. Such short-lived plants are good as a temporary hedge but should not be seen as a permanent feature of the landscape.

One of the most popular native plants for hedges is the rosemary grevillea (*Grevillea rosmarinifolia*) which has dense, prickly, bright green foliage that responds well to clipping. Regular cutting seems to prolong the plant's life. It must be grown in a spot with excellent drainage and is likely to succumb to root rot after periods of heavy rain. It is tolerant of quite cold conditions and appears to be more reliable in cool climates.

A better choice for warm coastal conditions could be some of the large flowered grevilleas with tropical ancestors. G. 'Robyn Gordon' and 'Superb' are long-flowering shrubs from warmer areas that can cope with more humid conditions. Their leaves are not as dense as those of the rosemary grevillea, which makes them unsuitable to clip into a formal hedge, but their decorative qualities are unrivalled.

Perhaps the best way to use grevilleas is as part of a mixed, informal screen, where it will not be so noticeable if a specimen is lost and has to be replaced.

One native that has been grown for many years as a clipped, squared-off hedge is the coast rosemary (*Westringia fruticosa*). It has grey-green foliage and pale mauve spring flowers that try to hide themselves among the crowded leaves. Because coast rosemary occurs naturally as a coastal heathland plant, it is able to stand up to all sorts of difficult conditions and can cope with periodic drought, salt winds and a wide range of temperatures.

Leptospermum scoparium var. *rotundifolium*, one of the native tea trees, grows in as many different conditions as the coast rosemary. Just as you would suspect, 'rotundifolium' means 'round leaves' and describes the shape of the foliage, but the size of the plant, and its flower colour, are quite variable. If you are using this tea tree for a formal hedge, then it is important to use cutting-grown stock from the one source. If left unclipped, the round-leafed tea tree can reach about one and a half metres but it is better cut to less than that after flowering has finished. The flowers are about 2.5 centimetres across, saucer-shaped and a white or pink shade.

Bottlebrush, too, seem remarkably unfussy about their situation and will survive in some horrible places but, of course, do better in good soil and with ample water. There is a popular form of bottlebrush (*Callistemon viminalis* 'Captain Cook') that has fine foliage and can be hedged at about one metre. The red flowers can appear at almost any time of year but are most prevalent in early summer, so it is best not to prune until after the main flush has finished. Other bottlebrushes are more suitable for taller screens.

If you wish to avoid pruning altogether, try growing a low hedge of long-leafed waxflower (*Eriostemon myoporoides*), whose main requirements are well-drained soil and at least half a day's sun. The starry, white flowers appear on the branches for a long time in late winter and spring. This plant tolerates a wide range of temperatures and mixes well with both natives and exotics. This easily grown native seems to be almost free of pests and looks good in place of a front fence.

Checklist: Low Hedges and Screens (1 to 1.5 m)

Flowering Hedges and Screens
Abelia × *grandiflora* **(Glossy Abelia)**
Height: 1.3 m.
Cut to: 1 m. Late winter.
Minimum Spacing: 40 cm.
Propagation: Semi-hardwood cuttings.
Comments: Hardy and attractive for almost all climates.

Brunfelsia bonodora **(Yesterday, Today and Tomorrow)**
Height: 3 m.
Cut to: 1.2 m. After flowering.
Minimum Spacing: 60 cm.
Propagation: Soft-tip cuttings spring and early summer. Seeds.
Comments: Frost-free districts.

Camellia hiemalis **'Shishi-gashira'**
C. hiemalis **'Showa-no-sakae'**   **(all known as Sasanqua**
C. sasanqua **'Mine-no-yuki'**   **Camellias)**
C. sasanqua **'Yuletide'**
Height: 2 m.
Cut to: 1 m. After flowering.
Minimum Spacing: 50 cm.
Propagation: Semi-hardwood cuttings. Air layers.
Comments: Grows in wide climatic range and in sun or shade.

Ceanothus × *veitchianus* 'Blue Pacific' (Californian Lilac)
Height: 3 m.
Cut to: 1.5 m. After flowering.
Minimum Spacing: 75 cm.
Propagation: Semi-hardwood cuttings.
Comments: Needs good drainage and freedom from summer humidity.

Chaenomeles speciosa (Japonica)
Height: 2 m.
Cut to: 1 m. After flowering.
Minimum Spacing: 50 cm.
Propagation: Hardwood cuttings in winter.
Comments: Deciduous. Flowers borne on bare branches in late winter.

Choisya ternata (Mexican Orange Blossom)
Height: 1.5 m.
Cut to: 1 m. After flowering.
Minimum Spacing: 50 cm.
Propagation: Semi-hardwood cuttings in late autumn.
Comments: Needs good drainage and freedom from summer humidity.

Coleonema pulchrum 'Nanum' (Dwarf Pink Diosma)
Height: 1.2 m.
Cut to: 1 m. Trim lightly after flowering.
Minimum Spacing: 30 cm.
Propagation: Soft-tip cuttings taken in spring.
Comments: Commence clipping plant when quite small. Must have good sun and drainage.

Escallonia rubra var. *macrantha* (Red-flowered Escallonia)
Height: 3 m.
Cut to: 1.2 m. In late winter.
Minimum Spacing: 60 cm.
Propagation: Semi-hardwood cuttings.
Comments: Will grow in a wide range of climates.

Hebe speciosa 'La Seduisante' (Hebe Veronica)
Height: 1 m.
Minimum Spacing: 50 cm.
Propagation: Semi-hardwood cuttings.
Comments: Trim off spent flowers. All hebes can tolerate some salt winds.

Ilex aquifolium (**English Holly**)
Height: 3 m.
Cut to: 1 m.
Minimum Spacing: 75 cm.
Propagation: Seed. Semi-hardwood cuttings.
Comments: Slow growing. Sun or semi-shade.

I. cornuta '**Rotunda**' (**Dwarf Chinese Holly**)
Height: 1 m.
Minimum Spacing: 50 cm.
Propagation: Semi-hardwood cuttings in early autumn.
Comments: Very slow growing cultivar. Useful for low barrier hedge.

Melastoma malabathricum (**Pink Lasiandra**)
Height: 2 m.
Cut to: 1.5 m. In early spring.
Minimum Spacing: 1 m.
Propagation: Semi-hardwood cuttings taken in late winter.
Comments: Use only in frost-free areas.

Plumbago auriculata (**Blue Plumbago**)
P. auriculata '*Alba*' (**White Plumbago**)
Height: 3 m.
Cut to: 1 m. Early spring.
Minimum Spacing: 50 cm.
Propagation: Tip cuttings taken spring to autumn.
Comments: Very fast growing.

Raphiolepis × *delacourii* (**Pink Indian Hawthorn**)
R. indica (**Indian Hawthorn**)
R. umbellata (**Japanese Hawthorn**)
Height: 1.5–3 m.
Cut to: 1 m. In summer, after main flowering.
Minimum Spacing: 50 cm.
Propagation: Semi-hardwood cuttings taken in autumn and early winter.
Comments: Slow growing but hardy plants.

Rhododendron azalea (**Tall, Single Azalea**)
'**Alba Magna**' (white); '**Alphonse Anderson**' (light and dark pink);
'**Magnifica**' (purple); '**Mauve Schryderi**' (light mauve); '**Mortii**'
(white)

Height: 2 m.
Cut to: 1 m. After flowering.
Minimum Spacing: 50 cm.
Propagation: Semi-hardwood cuttings. Ground layers.
Comments: Best in semi-shade but will tolerate full sun. Must have acid soil.

Spiraea cantoniensis 'Lanceata' (White May)
Height: 2.5 m.
Cut to: 1.2 m. After flowering.
Minimum Spacing: 60 cm.
Propagation: Semi-hardwood cuttings. Hardwood cuttings in winter. Division.
Comments: A deciduous shrub which must be cut back hard after spring flowering. At pruning time, remove some of the oldest canes at the base.

Strobilanthes anisophyllus (Goldfussia)
Height: 1.5 m.
Cut to: 1 m. After flowering.
Minimum Spacing: 50 cm.
Propagation: Semi-hardwood cuttings taken in autumn.
Comments: Will only tolerate very light frosts.

Tibouchina 'Jules' (Dwarf Tibouchina)
Height: 1 m.
Minimum Spacing: 50 cm.
Propagation: Tip cuttings taken in late summer and autumn.
Comments: Frost-free districts. Trim spent flowerheads.

Viburnum tinus (Laurustinus)
Height: 3 m.
Cut to: 1 m. In early spring after flowering.
Minimum Spacing: 60 cm.
Propagation: Semi-hardwood cuttings. Ground layers.
Comments: Very hardy.

Foliage Hedges and Screens
Acalypha wilkesiana (Fijian Fire Plant)
Height: 2 m.
Cut to: 1.5 m. In early spring.
Minimum Spacing: 75 cm.

Propagation: Tip cuttings taken from spring to autumn.
Comments: Frost-free districts.

Aucuba japonica 'Variegata' (Gold Dust Plant)
Height: 3 m.
Cut to: 1.5 m. In early spring.
Minimum Spacing: 60 cm.
Propagation: Tip cuttings in autumn and winter.
Comments: Very good for shade.

Berberis thunbergii 'Atropurpurea' (Purple Barberry)
Height: 2 m.
Cut to: 1 m. In late winter.
Minimum Spacing: 60 cm.
Propagation: Hardwood cuttings in winter.
Comments: Deciduous in winter. Spines on stems.

Buxus microphylla var. *japonica* (Japanese Box)
Height: 2 m.
Cut to: 1 m. Whenever necessary.
Minimum Spacing: 50 cm.
Propagation: Semi-hardwood cuttings.
Comments: Adapts well to geometric shearing.

B. sempervirens (English Box)
Height: 3 m.
Cut to: 1 m. Shear whenever necessary.
Minimum Spacing: 50 cm.
Propagation: Semi-hardwood cuttings.
Comments: Best in cooler climates.

Elaeagnus pungens 'Aurea' (Japanese Oleaster)
Height: 3 m.
Cut to: 1 m. In early spring.
Minimum Spacing: 60 cm
Propagation: Semi-hardwood cuttings.
Comments: Very hardy in wide climate range.

Euonymus japonicus (Japanese Spindle Bush)
Height: 3 m.
Cut to: 1 m. Late winter.

Minimum Spacing: 50 cm.
Propagation: Semi-hardwood cuttings.
Comments: Slow growing but hardy.

Nandina domestica (Japanese Sacred Bamboo)
Height: 2 m.
Minimum Spacing: 60 cm.
Propagation: Seed. Division in late winter.
Comments: Will grow in sun or shade. Loses some leaves in winter.
Spreads by means of suckers.

Photinia glabra 'Rubens' (Small-leafed Photinia)
Height: 3 m.
Cut to: 1 m. Whenever necessary.
Minimum Spacing: 50 cm.
Propagation: Semi-hardwood cuttings.
Comments: Frequent clipping promotes flushes of red, new growth.

Natives
Callistemon viminalis 'Captain Cook' (Captain Cook Bottlebrush)
Height: 2 m.
Cut to: 1 m. After flowering.
Minimum Spacing: 75 cm.
Propagation: Tip cuttings in late summer and autumn.
Comments: Red, brush flowers.

Eriostemon myoporoides (Long-leafed Waxflower)
Height: 1 m.
Minimum Spacing: 50 cm.
Propagation: Semi-hardwood cuttings.
Comments: Trim lightly after flowering.

Grevillea 'Robyn Gordon' (Robyn Gordon Grevillea)
Height: 1.2 m.
Cut to: 1 m. Trim flowered shoots.
Minimum Spacing: 50 cm.
Propagation: Semi-hardwood cuttings.
Comments: Light barrier hedge. Long flowering. Warm districts.

G. rosmarinifolia (Rosemary Grevillea)
Height: 2 m.
Cut to: 1 m. Whenever necessary.

Minimum Spacing: 50 cm.
Propagation: Semi-hardwood cuttings.
Comments: Cold hardy. Used as formal hedge but not always totally reliable.

G. 'Superb' (Superb Grevillea)
Height: 1.5 m.
Cut to: 1.2 m. After flowering.
Minimum Spacing: 75 cm.
Propagation: Semi-hardwood cuttings.
Comments: Light barrier hedge. Long flowering. Warm districts.

Leptospermum scoparium var. *rotundifolium* (Tea Tree)
Height: 1.5 m.
Cut to: 1 m. After flowering.
Minimum Spacing: 60 cm.
Propagation: Semi-hardwood cuttings.
Comments: Very open hedge. Must have good drainage.

Westringia fruticosa (Coast Rosemary)
Height: 1.5 m.
Cut to: 1 m. Whenever necessary.
Minimum Spacing: 50 cm.
Propagation: Semi-hardwood cuttings.
Comments: Excellent formal hedge.

Medium Hedges and Screens (1.5 to 3 m)

These are the real 'workhorses' of the garden because they do the main job of creating your private outdoor living areas. They make visual walls to protect you from a neighbour's prying eyes, they cut down traffic noise and they provide a soft background for lawns and garden beds. They all keep their foliage down to the ground with little or no clipping but they can be reduced to a particular size, or their foliage can be thickened, by regular pruning.

The Champions

These are the plants that have been tried and tested over many years and I have designated them 'champions' because they seem to do the best job of reliably and attractively screening off all or part of an outside landscape.

The first champion, the photinia, has been mentioned before. Photinias are tall-growing shrubs that produce clusters of tiny, white flowers in spring but are mostly grown for their bright red new leaves. If left uncut they will reach small tree size of four to five metres but are often pruned to approximately half that height. Two hybrids, *Photinia × fraseri* 'Robusta' and *P. × fraseri* 'Red Robin', are the most popular for screening work and are propagated from late autumn cuttings. 'Red Robin' appears to be the superior cultivar with its showy flushes of ruby red leaves.

Photinias seem able to survive almost any neglect but look at their best and brightest if they are well watered, fertilised and cut back a couple of times a year. Pruning encourages the development of colourful new shoots. The plants flourish in all but tropical areas.

A late starter in the championship stakes is the plant with no common name and a difficult botanical one, *Xylosma japonicum*. I am sure that people avoid buying this plant because they don't know how to pronounce its name but, if you remember that it starts off like xylophone, then the whole thing is much easier to say. It is a pity that the plant is not grown more widely because it is one of the best screening shrubs available. It grows naturally to somewhere between three and five metres or clips easily to much less.

Xylosma has pink new leaves that change to a shiny mid-green as they mature. The whole effect is of glossy, healthy, abundant growth. If uncut, the plant will develop a width of about three metres but this can easily be reduced to one metre without compromising on privacy. The flowers are an insignificant green and are hidden in the bush. It is happy in full sun or semi-shade and in almost any climate.

Two New Zealanders are found in the Hall of Champions. The first is variegated pittosporum (*Pittosporum eugenioides* 'Variegatum'), a densely foliaged shrub with cream markings in the edges of pale green leaves. Like the xylosma, it has almost unnoticeable flowers but is used for its striking foliage. I have been told that *P. eugenioides* looks stunning in its plain green form, but this appears to be unavailable in Australia.

Variegated pittosporum needs some basic care if it is to survive. It must have good drainage and regular, deep watering. It is susceptible to scale attack and may need to be treated with an anti-scale spray. Unlike most variegated plants, it seemed uninterested in reverting to its plain green form.

The other New Zealand champion is called New Zealand Christmas bush in Australia, but is known by the delightful Maori name of pohutukawa in its homeland. It blooms with bright orange or red, staminate flowers in the warmer months of the year. It is one of the toughest shrubs and is often found growing in its native habitat with its roots in salt water. Pohutukawa (*Metrosideros excelsa*) has fine grey hairs all over its new leaves and on the backs of the old leaves to help protect it from salt and pollution.

There are a few different types of New Zealand Christmas bush available and this seems to create a great deal of confusion about the various species, but they all come from the coastal fringes of the Pacific islands. One is a variegated form from the Kermadec islands (*M. kermadecensis* 'Variegata') that is commonly grown but is very reluctant to flower. However, it's still worth choosing just for its green and gold foliage.

Variegated pittosporum can cope with quite a cold position, but the New Zealand Christmas bush needs more protection from frosts. They can both grow to five metres in deep soil, but three metres of good cover is a more realistic expectation.

Another 'champion' that flourishes in cold areas is the cherry laurel (*Prunus laurocerasus*). This tall shrub comes as a surprise to anyone who is familiar with prunus as a deciduous flowering or fruiting tree because it has broad, glossy leaves that are evergreen and give good year-round protection to cool-climate gardens. The small, white, spring flowers come in 10-centimetre upright spikes and are followed by cherry-like fruit. Depending on soil depth, the plant will grow between three and five metres or can be clipped to much less. There is a similar evergreen prunus, Portuguese laurel (*P. lusitanica*) that is more suited to warm, dry climates. Both species make excellent hedges but are unhappy in coastal humidity.

The firethorns (*Pyracantha* species) are also seen at their best in cold districts where the low temperatures help develop good colour in the berries. Firethorns are evergreen and are armed with thorns which makes them useful barrier shrubs. They are often planted on farms to help confine animals to a particular paddock. The berries last for a long time in autumn and winter and are attractive to birds. *P. angustifolia*, with orange berries, and *P. coccinea*, with red berries, are two species that are popularly grown. They achieve much the same height as the cherry laurel and the variegated pittosporum, so could be used with these as an effective mixed screen in cool districts.

The native willow-leafed hakea (*Hakea salicifolia*) is another 'champion' screen plant that has been widely used in recent years. Its narrow leaves start off with a bronze coloration and gradually become medium green. The main appeal of this large shrub is its speedy growth, as it establishes very rapidly and can provide a quick screen. Unfortunately, the price that has to be paid for this speed is a fitting one — the plants are very short-lived and start to become thin and straggly after about eight years of growth.

You can prolong the useful life of willow-leafed hakea by pruning the plants at least once a year and by mulching and fertilising with a native plant fertiliser. Many gardeners take it for granted that these hakeas, like so many natives, prefer to grow in dry conditions but their native habitat can often be quite wet and they do not like to be stressed for water.

The best way of using willow-leafed hakea is as a 'nurse' screen. Plant a row of hakeas as a quick cover and, at the same time, put in some slower growing shrubs such as New Zealand Christmas bush.

The hakeas will grow quickly and 'nurse' the Christmas bush along until the hakeas can be taken out when the slower movers are a good size. This will only succeed if there is enough room for each row of plants to receive ample sunlight.

Some of the great screening plants are only suitable to use in a warm climate. One of the easiest is Cape honeysuckle (*Tecomaria capensis*) which grows as a sprawling, semi-climber to about three metres. It flowers all through summer and autumn with bright orange, tubular blooms. The establishment of this plant is so rapid that it can become an embarrassment as it clumps through the garden by means of suckering growths. It's not as bad as bamboo — you can mow it back — but be warned that it will spread and take on a life of its own. However, it's hard to beat as an attractive, tough screen or clipped hedge in frost-free districts and two annual prunings should keep it controlled. One advantage of its method of spreading is that the plant can be reproduced from the suckers, which makes propagation a simple matter.

Purple glory bush, or lasiandra (*Tibouchina* species), is another colourful shrub for subtropical and tropical regions. Tibouchinas are from warm parts of South America and have been selected and hybridised in recent years until there is a bewildering array of varieties, each with its special merits. Most of them flower in late summer and autumn in purple shades but there are white and pink blooming varieties. There is one that has been christened 'Noeline' and has white and pink flowers that change colour through various shades, in the manner of the yesterday, today and tomorrow bush.

The most suitable tibouchina to use for a two metre-high screen is the hybrid 'Alstonville' with its spectacular floral display and compact growth. All tibouchinas benefit from tip pruning while they develop and from a harder pruning after flowering. Like most subtropical plants, they are used to good rainfall so should be well watered and mulched.

I can't leave my 'Hall of Champions' without mentioning my two favourite hedging shrubs, *Murraya paniculata* and *Camellia sasanqua*.

M. paniculata is sometimes known as the cosmetic bark bush but the origins of this common name are rather obscure. Another name is orange jessamine, which seems more appropriate because the plants are in the same family as citrus and the flowers are reminiscent of orange blossom.

Murraya is a delightful plant that grows to between two and three metres or can be formally clipped to less than that. The scented white flowers come in flushes throughout summer and are followed by the occasional red fruit. Even without the blossoms, murraya would be worth growing for its beautiful, glossy foliage. It makes an excellent substitute for box in frost-free climates and the flowers are a bonus.

The new growth is a light, lime green and it gradually darkens as it ages. This gives the shrub an interesting two-toned effect during the growing period. The leaves are at their glossy best in some shade but it will grow happily in full sun.

All the murrayas come from South-East Asia, tropical Australia and the islands north of Australia. They are most suited to subtropical conditions with good watering but will take a very small amount of frost. *M. ovatifolia* is the native species that is difficult to obtain but is at least as attractive as the exotic murraya.

Sasanqua camellias have dark green, glossy leaves that look good all year round. They are wonderfully hardy plants that will tolerate city pollution or salt winds and will flourish in sun or shade. The autumn and early winter blooms look very delicate and come in soft shades of pink and white but, like the leaves, can stand up to harsh conditions. Some varieties have semi-double flowers but the classic sasanqua bloom is single with a centre of golden stamens.

Other camellia species will grow in a similar way and are also loosely termed 'sasanqua'. For a medium hedge, choose the upright growing types such as 'Plantation Pink', cerise 'Kanjiro' ('Hiryu'), white 'Setsugekka' or the semi-double pink 'Jennifer Susan'. It's a matter of personal taste whether you mix these varieties for a multi-coloured effect or unify your hedge by using one variety.

If your hedge is in a totally shaded area, you can use the slower growing japonica camellias. There are hundreds of cultivars to choose from but, for screening purposes, I would select one with relatively small leaves and flowers.

The williamsii hybrid camellias are credited with the most prolific blooming habit and the best known is the orchid pink 'Donation'. Like the sasanquas, they will grow in sun or shade but tend to suffer from dieback in humid districts.

Conifers

Conifers make up a large group of non-flowering plants that grow all over the world and come in a great variety of shapes and sizes. Some are especially popular for screening because their close, many-branched growth means that they create a dense 'wall' of foliage that can be impossible to see through. Many need to be pruned to restrain their size but it is important that any pruning is only carried out on the small, leafy twigs because, as a general rule, conifers are reluctant to re-shoot from the cut ends of woody branches. This means that pruning should be commenced long before the plant reaches the desired height.

Another important factor to consider when placing conifers in a landscape is that their growth habits can change according to the climate in which they are grown. The same species can be tall and narrow in a warm climate, or broad-spreading in a colder climate. One theory is that the trees develop a sweeping outline in order to shed the snow in cold areas. Whatever the reason, a conifer such as the bhutan cypress (*Cupressus torulosa*) can look like quite a different plant when seen in a different climatic zone.

Bhutan cypress is popular for a privacy screen and will grow to about eight or ten metres if left unclipped. However, if pruning is commenced early in the plant's life, it can be restricted to less than three metres. They are often kept at a height where a clipping routine can be followed without using a ladder.

The leaves are dark green and rather dull but make an attractive background for more flowery shrubs and perennials. There is a dwarf form available that stops at about two metres but it is rather hard to obtain and grows very slowly. Bhutan cypress is very narrow in frost-free climates but becomes much taller and wider in cold districts.

Another conifer that grows in a similar manner is the Brunnings golden cypress (*C. macrocarpa* 'Brunniana'). At one time this form of the Californian monterey cypress was considered to be the ideal plant for a screen with its close, bright yellow leaves and rapid growth, and they were planted profusely. Unfortunately, once established, they were found to be susceptible to many pests and diseases which caused dieback and death. You can imagine the frustration of the homeowner who has just established a complete barrier, only to find that one or two of the plants in the row have died! A regular feeding and watering program will help sustain some of the trees but this variety is not recommended for a single species screen.

Leyland cypress, the conifer that is now grown in place of the Brunnings cypress, seems to be an altogether tougher customer. It is a bigeneric cross between two different plants, which means that the

botanic name is written as × *Cupressocyparis leylandii*, and it appears
to have inherited the best features of both its parents. It has the speedy
growth and attractiveness of the monterey cypress (*Cupressus macrocarpa*)
but is strengthened by the hardiness of its other parent, the Alaskan
nootka cypress, *Chamaecyparis nootkatensis*. These two plants seem to
represent the different lifestyles of the people from their respective
homelands — the free and easy Californian coastal party-goers
contrasted with the Eskimos' serious and purposeful approach to life!
The nootka cypress is one of the few conifers that will cope with poor
drainage and some of this characteristic has been inherited by the leyland
cypress.

Leyland cypress comes in many forms and colours. The most popular
is 'Castlewellan Gold', which has lime coloured foliage and develops
an upright habit. 'Green Spire' and 'Naylor's Blue' have even narrower
growth while 'Leighton's Green' is more spreading. All the leyland
cypress have been popular for years in Europe because of their hardiness
and rapid development. In a happy situation they will grow at least
a metre in a year and they thrive in a wide climatic range. If left
untrimmed they will reach ten metres but are successful if kept to much
less than that.

The more patient gardener can use the classic English hedging plant,
the yew (*Taxus baccata*). This is an unusual conifer because, rather than
a cone, it produces a fleshy fruit which is said to be poisonous. Yews
are very long-lived and for centuries have been clipped and trained
in European gardens. They have been popularly used for cutting to
shape as topiary as well as for hedges. They have very dark green,
sombre foliage and, fittingly, are most often seen surrounding
churchyards and cemeteries. Don't let this put you off, however, because
yews are also found enclosing some of the world's greatest gardens and
a yew hedge is very socially acceptable. Yew is only successful in cool
climates with adequate rainfall but can be used in sun or shade.

If you want a similar effect in a warmer climate, then try some of
the plum pines (*Podocarpus* species). There is a native from the east coast
rainforests that is called the Illawarra plum (*P. elatus*) and has been
grown for many years as a hedge as far south as Melbourne, or there
is a similar African species (*P. falcatus*) with narrower, dark green leaves.
Both are capable of growing to large tree height but they do this slowly
so can be easily restricted to shrub size, as long as cutting is commenced
early in their life.

Callistemon viminalis 'Captain Cook' makes a good low-growing native hedge.

Dwarf form of the native lilly pilly.

Nandina: an adaptable low screening plant.

Traditional clipped box hedge.

New red growth is a feature of photinea.

Azaleas will form a low hedge with a great spring show.

Colourful *Tibouchina* 'Alstonville' will form a medium hedge.

Pigeon berry will attract birds.

Semi-hardwood murraya cuttings (see pp. 9–11).

Murraya is a good choice for a medium clipped hedge.

Natives

Many Australian native plants have a 'short life but a gay one' and, as mentioned before, are only suitable as 'quick-fix' screens. This applies to the willow-leafed hakea already described (see page 44), and to the grevilleas, or spider flowers.

There are hundreds of species of grevilleas that grow naturally in the bush and they are being hybridised all the time to produce more varieties. They have small, individual flowers grouped together in three basic types: spider, toothbrush or bottlebrush. The bottlebrush flowers are usually seen only in warm areas while the spider and toothbrush types will handle much colder climates. Nearly all of them tend to fade out after about ten years although their lives can be prolonged by frequent, light clipping, especially after flowering. They do not make a very dense screen so do not use where a complete block is desired.

G. longifolia, *G. hookeriana* and *G.* 'Ivanhoe' are three red, toothbrush-flowered varieties that grow to between two and three metres and, if occasionally cut back, will perform particularly well as fence plants. One added bonus is that their flowers are very attractive to honey-eating birds. Their blooming period lasts for a long time through winter, spring and summer.

The warm climate bottlebrush grevilleas usually have deeply cut leaves and make a very light visual barrier. Their main feature, the racemes of showy flowers, can be seen all year round. One particularly fine example is *G.* 'Honey Gem' with honeycomb coloured clusters of flowers. 'Moonlight' has pale cream floral sprays while the red Banks' grevillea (*G. banksii*), which normally grows as a small tree, can be trimmed to stay shrubby and proves another fine example of the bottlebrush type.

Most of the spider-flowered grevilleas have small, close growth that clips well and reveals the clusters of flowers. They are best if trimmed hard and kept to a height that is less than 1.5 metres, as the constant cutting seems to prolong their life. *G. glabrata*, with white, lacy blooms, could be trained up to two metres and still retain good, dense growth.

Melaleucas can be used as a quick screen and are versatile because they are adaptable to almost any soil. Most will stand periods of poor drainage. *Melaleuca bracteata* 'Revolution Green' and 'Revolution Gold' can both be kept at two or three metres and with their fine leaves will perform an effective screening function.

'Revolution Green' has fresh, bright green foliage while 'Revolution Gold' is golden yellow, reminiscent of some of the golden conifers. They do have white summer flowers but these are secondary in importance to the foliage. The leaves can be attacked by native, leaf-eating caterpillars which are easily removed by hand when first seen, but can cause rapid defoliation if unnoticed.

M. decussata will grow to just the right height without being trimmed and has pretty mauve spring and summer flowers. Unfortunately, these flowers fade to a rather dingy, off-white that slightly spoils the appearance of the shrub. *M. diosmifolia* grows to a similar height and has unusual lime-green blooms but is only suitable for frost-free districts. *M. incana* has very grey leaves that contrast with the yellow, brush flowers, but seems to be irresistibly attractive to pests.

The best screening bottlebrush in this size range is *Callistemon citrinus* 'Endeavour' with stiff, lemon-scented leaves and naturally thick growth. It can handle almost anything: wind, frost, salt, and poor drainage. If the spent red bottlebrushes are cut off when finished then the growth will remain bushy and the unattractive seed pods will not form. These seed pods can persist for years in the hope that a fire will come along and force them to open. You can achieve the same effect by baking them in the oven until they spill their fine seeds.

C. citrinus 'Endeavour' can be interplanted with *C. paludosus*, which has creamy-white flowers, if a colour variation is desired. Their growth habits are not identical but it only takes some light pruning to persuade them into a similar shape.

Many of the tea trees (*Leptospermum* species) are too easily attacked by pests to make a good screen but one, the lemon-scented tea tree (*Leptospermum petersonii*) is protected from attack by the lemon-sherbet fragrance of the leaves. If left unpruned, lemon-scented tea tree will grow to a tree-like four metres but will stay shrubby in growth if clipped at less than that. It has pretty, white, spring and summer flowers and thrives in almost any area without heavy frosts.

One of my favourite natives for hedging is the narrow-leafed lilly pilly (*Acmena smithii* var. *minor*). It has developed in creek beds where it is subjected to regular flooding and this has stunted its growth. It retains its dwarf characteristics when grown from seed or cuttings, even if it is planted in a more congenial position.

Narrow-leaved lilly pilly has all the desirable characteristics of its big brother, the full sized lilly pilly. It has dense, shiny leaves, pink new growth and showy winter fruits that range in colour from soft pink to mauve. It will grow in sun or shade, handle light frosts and stand periods of poor drainage. If uncut, it will reach between three and four metres.

Flowering Hedges

Although not as dense and tidy as the plants listed as 'The Champions', these flowering screeners are useful because they are speedy and attractive and their somewhat floppy growth helps to avoid a regimented look in the garden.

In warm areas pigeon berry (*Duranta erecta*) can either be left to grow informally to three or four metres or clipped to shape at much less. This is an excellent year-round shrub with good-looking leaves, clusters of lilac-blue flowers in summer and autumn, and orange berries that will last through to winter if not eaten by greedy birds. It is not often seen in nurseries — for some reason it is out of fashion — but strikes very easily from semi-hardwood cuttings in autumn. The branches carry small spines which make an effective barrier.

In the tropics and subtropics the word 'hedge' is almost synonymous with evergreen hibiscus (*Hibiscus rosa-sinensis*). These plants originally came from Asia but have been planted so extensively through the Pacific islands that they have naturalised themselves and many varieties are now called 'Hawaiian' or 'Fijian'. There is a bewildering array of flower colours and plant sizes and it is important that, for a mixed hibiscus hedge, varieties should be selected that grow to a similar size. They are often classified as small (less than 1.5 metres), medium (two to three metres), and tall (more than three metres).

'Catavki' which is bright red, 'Brucei' which is yellow, and 'Celia' with apricot and pink blooms, are three single-flowered medium growers that would mix well to form a colourful unclipped hedge. You may be setting yourself on a frustrating course, however, if you go along to a nursery armed with a list of cultivar names. It is better to decide on a size range and select plants with appealing blooms that fit into that particular range.

Evergreen hibiscus need to be in a frost-free spot with good watering and excellent drainage. The hardiest types are the big growing singles such as 'Apple Blossom', 'Agnes Galt' and 'Wilder's White'. They are often clipped into a more formal hedge and this keeps their growth thick and leafy. The best time to prune hibiscus hedges is in the spring; avoid pruning in autumn or winter.

Hibiscus are susceptible to a number of insect pests and fungus diseases and are sensitive to many of the commonly used insecticides. Make sure that you use pesticides that are labelled as being suitable for hibiscus and encourage healthy growth by good watering, mulching and fertilising.

Rondeletia amoena is also for frost-free gardens and makes an attractive informal screen. *Amoena* means 'lovely' and, indeed, the clusters of salmon-pink spring blooms are just that. Rondeletia is too twiggy for formal hedging but benefits from a hard cutting in late spring after the major flowering period. It needs a sunny position that is sheltered from cold winds.

The butterfly bush (*Buddleia davidii*) is delightfully unfussy about climate and will grow almost anywhere. This is the screening plant to choose if you want a fast grower that sends up arching growths tipped with lilac-purple flower sprays. These summer flowers have a strong, polleny perfume that is irresistibly attractive to butterflies. It can be rather a messy shrub and benefits from hard cutting after the flowers have finished, but it can make a two metre high screen in two growing seasons.

In cold climates, your choice includes the Californian native catkin bush (*Garrya elliptica*) with long, yellow, tassel flowers that hang from the bush like drooping necklaces. This evergreen grows to about 2.5 metres and flowers in winter. It dislikes summer humidity and tends to fade away in coastal districts but is reliable in inland areas as long as it is well watered. The male form is vastly superior to the female so it should always be reproduced by cuttings taken from proven performers.

Checklist: Medium Hedges and Screens (1.5 to 3 m)

The Champions
Camellia japonica (Japonica Camellia)
Height: 4 m.

Minimum Spacing: 1.2 m.
Propagation: Semi-hardwood cuttings in autumn. Air layers.
Comments: Best in semi-shade.

C. hiemalis '**Kanjiro**' or '**Hiryu**'
C. sasanqua '**Jennifer Susan**'   (**all known as Sasanqua**
C. sasanqua '**Plantation Pink**'   **Camellias**)
C. sasanqua '**Setsugekka**'
Height: 4 m.
Cut to: 1.5 m. After flowering.
Minimum Spacing: 1 m.
Propagation: Semi-hardwood cuttings. Air layers.
Comments: Winter blooming. Will handle some salt.

C. × *williamsii* '**Donation**' (**Donation Camellia**)
Height: 3 m.
Cut to: 2 m.
Minimum Spacing: 1 m.
Propagation: Semi-hardwood cuttings. Air layers.
Comments: Free flowering. Not for humid areas.

Hakea salicifolia (**Willow-leafed Hakea**)
Height: 5 m.
Cut to: 2 m. Whenever necessary.
Minimum Spacing: 1.5 m.
Propagation: Seed.
Comments: Fast growing but short-lived.

Metrosideros excelsa (**NZ Christmas Bush**)
Height: 5 m.
Cut to: 2 m. At end of winter.
Minimum Spacing: 1.5 m.
Propagation: Seed; semi-hardwood cuttings.
Comments: Hardy and salt resistant.

M. kermadecensis '**Variegata**' (**Variegated NZ Christmas Bush**)
Height: 3 m.
Cut to: 2 m. End of winter.
Minimum Spacing: 1.5 m.
Propagation: Semi-hardwood cuttings.
Comments: Reluctant to flower.

Murraya paniculata (**Orange Jessamine**)
Height: 3 m.
Cut to: 1.5 m. After autumn flowering. Can be lightly sheared at any time of year.
Minimum Spacing: 75 cm.
Propagation: Semi-hardwood cuttings.
Comments: Good formal hedge. *M. ovatifolia* is a hard-to-find native species.

Photinia × *fraseri* '**Red Robin**' (**Photinia**)
P. × *fraseri* '**Robusta**'
Height: 4 m.
Cut to: 2 m. Late winter.
Minimum Spacing: 1 m.
Propagation: Semi-hardwood cuttings.
Comments: Prune with secateurs. Don't shear.

Pittosporum eugenioides '**Variegatum**' (**Variegated Pittosporum**)
Height: 4 m.
Cut to: 2 m. Late winter.
Minimum Spacing: 1 m.
Propagation: Semi-hardwood tip cuttings.
Comments: Grows in wide climate range.

Prunus laurocerasus (**Cherry Laurel**)
P. lusitanica (**Portuguese Laurel**)
Height: 4 m.
Cut to: 2 m. After spring flowering.
Minimum Spacing: 1 m.
Propagation: Semi-hardwood cuttings. Seed.
Comments: Trim with secateurs. Don't shear. Portuguese laurel will stand hotter, drier conditions.

Pyracantha angustifolia (**Orange Firethorn**)
P. coccinea (**Red Firethorn**)
Height: 3 m.
Cut to: 1.5 m. Only cut shoots that have berried.
Minimum Spacing: 1 m.
Propagation: Seed.
Comments: Very hardy in wide climate range. Best show in cold districts.

Tecomaria capensis (**Cape Honeysuckle**)
Height: 3 m.

Cut to: 1.5 m. Early spring.
Minimum Spacing: 1 m.
Propagation: Semi-hardwood cuttings. Ground layers. Division.
Comments: Frost-free districts.

Tibouchina 'Alstonville' **(Lasiandra)**
T. **'Noeline' (Bicoloured Lasiandra)**
Height: 3 m.
Cut to: 2 m. After flowering or in late winter.
Minimum Spacing: 1.2 m.
Propagation: Tip cuttings all year.
Comments: Frost-free districts.

Xylosma japonicum **(Shiny Xylosma)**
Height: 4 m.
Cut to: 1.5 m. Any time of year.
Minimum Spacing: 75 cm.
Propagation: Semi-hardwood tip cuttings.
Comments: Excellent screen for all but coldest districts.

Conifers
x *Cupressocyparis leylandii* **(Leyland Cypress)**
Height: 10 m.
Cut to: 2 m. At any time of year.
Minimum Spacing: 1 m.
Propagation: Semi-hardwood cuttings.
Comments: Suitable for shearing as formal hedge. Coloured forms available
are 'Castlewellan Gold', 'Naylor's Blue', 'Leighton's Green'.

Cupressus macrocarpa 'Brunniana' **(Brunning's Golden Cypress)**
Height: 10 m.
Cut to: 2 m. At any time of year.
Minimum Spacing: 1 m.
Propagation: Semi-hardwood cuttings.
Comments: Prone to borers and fungal disease.

C. torulosa **(Bhutan Cypress)**
Height: 10 m.
Cut to: 2 m. At any time of year.
Minimum Spacing: 1 m.
Propagation: Semi-hardwood cuttings.
Comments: Needs good care if closely planted.

Podocarpus elatus (Illawarra Plum)
P. falcatus (Plum Pine)
Height: 10 m.
Cut to: 2 m. At any time of year.
Minimum Spacing: 1 m.
Propagation: Seed.
Comments: Grown as warm climate substitute for English yew. P. elatus is an Australian native.

Taxus baccata (English Yew)
Height: 10 m.
Cut to: 2 m.
Minimum Spacing: 1 m.
Propagation: Semi-hardwood cuttings.
Comments: Slow-growing English hedge plant.

Natives
Acmena smithii var. *minor* (Narrow-leafed Lilly Pilly)
Height: 4 m.
Cut to: 2 m. Late winter.
Minimum Spacing: 1 m.
Propagation: Semi-hardwood cuttings. Seed.
Comments: Trimming promotes flushes of pink, new growth.

Callistemon citrinus 'Endeavour' (Endeavour Bottlebrush)
Height: 3 m.
Cut to: 1.5 m. After flowering.
Minimum Spacing: 75 cm.
Propagation: Semi-hardwood tip cuttings.
Comments: Hardy in almost any climate. *C. paludosus*, with cream flowers, makes a good colour contrast but must be pruned regularly to keep compact.

Grevillea banksii (Bottlebrush Grevillea)
G. 'Honey Gem'
G. 'Moonlight'
Height: 3 m.
Cut to: 2 m. Remove spent flower spikes.
Minimum Spacing: 1 m.
Propagation: Semi-hardwood cuttings.
Comments: Light, see-through screen for warm climates.

G. glabrata (**White Spider Flower**)
Height: 3 m.
Cut to: 1.5 m. After flowering.
Minimum Spacing: 1.2 m.
Propagation: Semi-hardwood cuttings.
Comments: Needs good drainage but grows in a wide climate range.

G. hookeriana (**Toothbrush Grevillea**)
G. '**Ivanhoe**'
G. longifolia
Height: 2–3 m.
Cut to: 2 m. After flowering.
Minimum Spacing: 1 m.
Propagation: Semi-hardwood tip cuttings.
Comments: Light screen for a range of climates.

Leptospermum petersonii (**Lemon-scented Tea Tree**)
Height: 4 m.
Cut to: 2 m. After flowering.
Minimum Spacing: 1 m.
Propagation: Semi-hardwood cuttings. Seed.
Comments: All but coldest areas.

Melaleuca bracteata '**Revolution Gold**' (**Golden Melaleuca**)
M. bracteata '**Revolution Green**' (**Green Melaleuca**)
Height: 3 m.
Cut to: 1.5 m. Late winter.
Minimum Spacing: 75 cm.
Propagation: Semi-hardwood cuttings.
Comments: 'Revolution Green' is more cold hardy.

M. decussata (**Mauve Melaleuca**)
Height: 2 m.
Cut to: 1.5 m. After flowering.
Minimum Spacing: 75 cm.
Propagation: Semi-hardwood cuttings. Seed.
Comments: Very hardy. *M. diosmifolia*, with green flowers, is suitable for frost-free districts.

M. incana (**Grey Honey Myrtle**)
Height: 3 m.

Cut to: 1.5 m. After flowering.
Minimum Spacing: 1 m.
Propagation: Seed.
Comments: Frequently troubled by insect pests.

Flowering Hedges and Screens
Buddleia davidii **(Butterfly Bush)**
Height: 3 m.
Cut to: 2 m. Late winter.
Minimum Spacing: 1 m.
Propagation: Semi-hardwood cuttings.
Comments: Fast growing. Untidy.

Duranta erecta **(Pigeon Berry)**
Height: 4 m.
Cut to: 1.5 m. Late winter.
Minimum Spacing: 75 cm.
Propagation: Semi-hardwood cuttings.
Comments: Can be regularly pruned as a formal hedge. Frost-free districts.

Garrya elliptica **(Catkin Bush)**
Height: 3 m.
Cut to: 2.5 m. After flowering.
Minimum Spacing: 1 m.
Propagation: Semi-hardwood cuttings.
Comments: Best in areas with cold winters.

Hibiscus rosa-sinensis **'Brucei', 'Catavki', 'Celia' (Hibiscus)**
Height: 2–3 m.
Cut to: 2 m. Early spring.
Minimum Spacing: 75 cm.
Propagation: Semi-hardwood cuttings.
Comments: Frost-free districts.

H. rosa-sinensis **'Agnes Galt', 'Apple Blossom', 'Wilder's White' (Tall Hibiscus)**
Height: 3–4 m.
Cut to: 2 m. Early spring.
Minimum Spacing: 1 m.
Propagation: Semi-hardwood cuttings.
Comments: Frost-free districts.

Rondeletia amoena **(Pink Rondeletia)**
Height: 3 m.
Cut to: 2 m. After flowering.
Minimum Spacing: 1 m.
Propagation: Semi-hardwood cuttings, late spring (ie. at pruning time.)
Comments: Frost-free districts.

Tall Screens (more than 3 m)

Many of the plants already suggested for medium hedges will make a large screen if left unclipped. Variegated pittosporum (*Pittosporum eugenioides* 'Variegatum') can form a dense hedge to five metres in happy conditions. Photinias can also get close to tree size, but look thicker and display more of their red leaves if regularly pruned. Cherry laurels will reach five metres if grown in a moist, cool climate but are most often seen clipped to much less than that. It's a matter of deciding what suits your garden and meets your screening needs.

In small gardens, formal tall hedges can look quite boring and can create a 'closed-in' effect. Most of the plants suggested in this section will look better if planted as part of a mixed screen, rather than having a row of a single species. You can get away with a more formal tall hedge in a large garden but you may still like to use the softening effect of a mixed, informal screen.

Natives

Australian native plants are often the best choice for creating large screens because they have evolved to handle the poor soils and low rainfall of this continent. Local natives are the easiest to grow; if you choose plants from other parts of the country you will have to regard them as another type of exotic, and adjust their conditions accordingly.

Some of the best trees to use when creating a large barrier are those from the east coast rainforests. Many of these are giants in their natural habitat but achieve less than half their possible size when grown in garden conditions.

My favourites are the lilly pillies, with their shiny leaves and pink or red new growth. The full-sized form of *Acmena smithii* grows to about seven metres in gardens and looks a picture in autumn when it develops its pink fruit. These berries are attractive to birds and can be eaten straight off the tree or used for making jellies and jams.

This lilly pilly can handle light frosts but may lose some new leaves in the colder weather. It is often attacked by scale insects and this causes sooty mould to grow on the leaf surfaces. While the trees are young it is practical to spray with an anti-scale spray but this becomes more difficult as they grow taller. Once the scale insects are destroyed, the sooty mould flakes off of its own accord.

Most of the lilly pillies used to be grouped in the genus *Eugenia* but botanists have separated them into many different (and confusing) genera. *Waterhousia floribunda* is a big growing lilly pilly that reaches 10 metres in gardens and has beautiful weeping branchlets. It is sometimes still listed under its old names of *Eugenia ventenattii* or *Syzygium floribundum*. It has a profuse flowering which is followed by a heavy crop of pale green fruit.

The riberry (*Syzygium leuhmannii*) seems to have a botanic name that is more like a spelling test, which hardly does justice to its beauty. 'Syzygium' is derived from an astronomical term which refers to the conjunction of two heavenly bodies and has been chosen, in this case, because the plant's two emerging seed-leaves are joined together after germination. Don't let its name distract you from appreciating the qualities of the plant, however, as many people consider riberry to be the pick of the lilly pillies. It has a distinctly weeping habit, bright pink new leaves, and red, pear-shaped fruit. It usually only reaches large shrub size in cultivation and stays branched right down to the ground. All these lilly pillies like warm positions with no more than very light frosts and plenty of water.

A good companion for the lilly pillies is the ivory curl flower (*Buckinghamia celsissima*). It is a rainforest plant with dense foliage that can adjust to life as far south as Melbourne. Curiously, the plant's ultimate size diminishes as it moves further south. The thin leaves on a young plant can look unattractive but they become broader and lusher as the tree grows. 'Ivory curl' aptly describes the cream flower clusters that decorate this tree in late summer.

Some of the subtropical rainforest plants can be established in areas with moderately heavy frosts, particularly if given protection when young. One example is the lemon-scented myrtle (*Backhousia citriodora*) which grows to a bushy small tree of about 6 metres and uses the lemon-like oil in its leaves to protect itself from insect attack. Another popular choice is the blueberry ash (*Elaeocarpus reticulatus*) which is an upright grower that is decorated with white or pink fringed bell flowers that are followed by shiny, blue fruit.

Queensland pittosporum grows in a similar upright manner to the lemon-scented myrtle and is at its best in autumn when covered by the bright orange berries that follow the white summer flowers. Lemon-scented myrtle, blueberry ash, riberry, ivory curl flower and Queensland pittosporum would make a dense, mixed, informal screen if planted about two metres apart and given good care.

Pittosporum undulatum, the native daphne, usually grows between five and seven metres tall and has glossy green leaves that are sometimes dimpled by an insect pest. The spring flowers have a beautiful perfume and the tree grows happily in areas with no more than light frosts. The flowers are followed by showy orange fruit containing seeds that sometimes germinate too easily. Because of its free-seeding qualities, native daphne has acquired a bad reputation and is not used as widely as it used to be. It can be replaced in the dry inland by its fine-leafed relative, the butterbush (*P. phillyreoides*).

There is a wattle to be found for every situation and they are often used as a quick 'nurse' screen. One of the most versatile is the Sydney golden wattle (*Acacia longifolia*) which thrives in a wide range of climates and positions. Another attractive small tree is the weeping sticky wattle (*A. howittii*) with small, sickle-shaped, shiny green leaves that are covered with hairs that give them the characteristic 'sticky' feel. For inland positions, the slightly larger Cootamundra wattle (*A. baileyana*) is widely planted and makes a great show in late winter when the bright yellow flowers contrast with the blue-grey foliage. There is a cultivated form of the Cootamundra wattle that has purple new growth and purple seed pods (*A. baileyana* 'Purpurea') which produces an even more marked colour contrast.

All of these wattles are short-lived and are unlikely to provide useful cover for more than ten years, although frequent pruning seems to prolong their lives. They are unrivalled, however, for creating a quick, attractive screen that can be regularly replanted or used while other, slower trees are developing.

The great virtue, too, of the bracelet honey myrtle (*Melaleuca armillaris*) is its speed of growth and its ability to provide quick cover, but I don't think it has much else going for it. Of course, it is very tough and tolerant of difficult soils and strong winds but its fine foliage is often reduced by insect attack. It has been overused by many local authorities and a friend of mine expresses the way it has worn out its welcome by describing it as 'that highway plant'. Like the wattles, its life can be lengthened by regular pruning.

At least two of the bottlebrushes are popularly used as a tall screen. Weeping bottlebrush (*Callistemon viminalis*) is most commonly available in its selected cultivar 'Hannah Ray' and grows to about five metres. It has fine, drooping branches that are decorated with red, brush flowers in spring. It thrives in a wide range of climates and will tolerate periods of water-logging.

The growth of weeping bottlebrush is too thin to make a solid screen and that job is best left to another species, the willow bottlebrush (*C. salignus*). 'Salignus' means 'willow-like', but in this case refers to the shape of the leaves rather than the habit of the tree. Willow bottlebrush has upright growth to about six metres and makes an excellent dense screen in areas without heavy frost. It can take a few years to produce its first show of cream, brush blooms but is decorated in spring from a young age by the distinctly pink new shoots that gradually turn green as they age. This characteristic has given rise to another common name — 'pink tips'. There is a red-flowered form available but I think that the rich red of the blooms contrasts rather strangely with the pink, new growth.

Another tree with a weeping habit is the Western Australian willow myrtle (*Agonis flexuosa*). This small (to about six metres) tree has drooping branches and fine, willow-like leaves. The alternate leaf arrangement causes the new stems to grow in a curious zig-zag formation. The new leaves are a light red and the small spring flowers are white. Willow myrtle will not survive heavy frosts but can handle drought once well established. As part of a screen it would need to be underplanted with lower shrubs which would cover the bare trunk.

Wilga (*Geijera parviflora*) is an excellent weeping tree which usually grows to about six metres and does well in the dry inland. Its fine foliage is very dense and it branches from near the ground. It is fairly cold tolerant and has sprays of cream flowers but may take some time to flower as it is quite slow growing. It's an Australian native that seems to have been more used and appreciated overseas than in its homeland.

Banksia ericifolia, the heath banksia, is another moderately slow grower that is suitable as a large screen and is well worth waiting for. It has fine, almost needle-like, foliage and orange flower spikes in autumn and winter. It needs good drainage but will grow in quite cold areas. Its best features are magnified in the hybrid cultivar 'Giant Candles' which first occurred in a Brisbane garden and has been spread all over the country. The flower spikes in 'Giant Candles'' can be 40 centimetres long and are irresistibly attractive to honeyeaters.

Exotics

Some of our best garden screeners come from across the Tasman. They include the New Zealand Christmas bush and the variegated pittosporum already mentioned (both of which make a large screen if left unclipped), but there are other New Zealand plants that are worth considering as part of a hedge or a mixed screen. One very rapid grower, *Pittosporum tenuifolium* 'James Stirling', quickly reaches four metres and gives a delicate effect, with its fine black stems and round, silvery-grey foliage. It is a great fence plant because of its upright habit which seldom becomes more than two metres wide. It needs good drainage but seems very cold hardy and will grow in sun or semi-shade.

Another New Zealander, the lace bark, is little known and deserves to be more widely grown. Lace bark (*Hoheria populnea*) grows quickly to about five metres, although there are variegated forms that are smaller than this. The name 'lace bark' refers to the lacy pattern of the layer of inner bark which was used by the Maoris to make cloths and string. The medium-sized leaves look so fresh and soft that one would swear it was a deciduous tree with a new crop of foliage. These leaves have toothed edges and make a pleasant background for the starry, white, summer flowers. Lace bark may be a little hard to find but is definitely worth hunting around for. It is hardy in cold conditions but will not tolerate drought.

Irish strawberry (*Arbutus unedo*) is an interesting European tree that grows in most climates. Its display is best in cold areas that bring out good colours in the winter fruit. At the same time as the fruit is ripening, the next season's crop of white, bell-shaped flowers is forming, which makes the tree a delight in the depths of winter. The hard leaves can stand up to sun, wind and cold. Irish strawberry grows a little slowly and will eventually reach five metres.

From the other side of the world comes the lance-leaf azara (*Azara lanceolata*). This is a tall Chilean shrub with small foliage and perfumed, inconspicuous yellow flowers. It would not be dense enough to use as

Camellia sasanqua 'Yuletide'.

'Apple Blossom' makes a hardy, medium-sized hibiscus hedge.

Cape honeysuckle will quickly form a 3-metre-high screen.

Sasanqua camellias make low to medium hedges and give winter colour.

Waterhousia floribunda (weeping lilly pilly) is an adaptable tall screening plant.

Hardy NZ Christmas bush
(*Metrosideros excelsa*).

Ivory curl flower.

Lavender does well on the coast.

The native coast rosemary (Westringia fruticosa) is a hardy seaside plant.

a single species screen but could be useful in a mixed shrubbery along a fenceline. It grows to about five metres and does best in cooler districts.

Conifers

Conifers such as Bhutan cypress and the leyland cypress will reach ten metres if they are left unclipped and grown in good soil and conditions. Once they grow higher than two metres, clipping them becomes a much more difficult exercise, involving ladders, planks and scaffolding, and should only be contemplated if you are very rich or very patient. Some other conifers will stop at lesser heights but remember that their growth can vary enormously, depending on the climate.

One of the most popular in warm regions is the Cripp's golden cypress (*Chamaecyparis obtusa* 'Crippsii') which grows in a fat conical shape to about four metres. The flat sprays of bright yellow growth occur all over the outside of the plant and provide an interesting colour contrast with any dark-green leaves. This golden colouring is lost if the plant is grown in the shade.

In old age, Cripp's golden cypress can reach more than five metres but it will take a long time before it gets to that height. Unlike many conifers, it is reliable in humid climates but is definitely for the patient.

Humidity doesn't seem to worry the keteleer juniper (*Juniperus chinensis* 'Keteleeri') either. It grows to five metres with dark green, sombre foliage and an upright, slightly ragged outline. Because of this uneven silhouette, it is best in a mixed screen rather than one composed of a single species.

Thuja plicata 'Zebrina' is a form of the American western red cedar with gold tips on its sprays of foliage. In most Australian conditions it only reaches tall shrub size, but in colder districts with deep soil it may become much bigger and wider. It is a very hardy plant which will grow happily in inland districts (if given summer water), or in coastal humidity.

All these conifers need to be planted in sunny positions and will tend to lose foliage if grown in too much shade. For more sheltered conditions, use the plum pines (*Podocarpus* species) which don't mind growing in about half-day sun.

Checklist: Tall Screens (more than 3 m)

Natives
Acacia baileyana (**Cootamundra Wattle**)
Height: 6 m.
Minimum Spacing: 2 m.
Propagation: Seed. Scarify by pouring boiling water on seeds and allow to cool before sowing.
Comments: Fast-growing and short-lived. There is an attractive form with purple new leaves and fruit — *A. baileyana* 'Purpurea'.

A. *howittii* (Sticky Wattle)
Height: 5 m.
Minimum Spacing: 2 m.
Propagation: Seed. Scarify as above.
Comments: Fast growing and short-lived in a wide range of conditions.

A. *longifolia* (Sydney Golden Wattle)
Height: 5 m.
Minimum Spacing: 1.5 m.
Propagation: Seed. Scarify as above.
Comments: Fast growing and short-lived.

***Acmena smithii* (Lilly Pilly)**
Height: 7–10 m in gardens.
Minimum Spacing: 2 m.
Propagation: Seed.
Comments: Reliable and attractive.

***Agonis flexuosa* (WA Weeping Myrtle)**
Height: 6 m.
Minimum Spacing: 2 m.
Propagation: Seed.
Comments: Single trunk and weeping head.

***Backhousia citriodora* (Lemon-scented Myrtle)**
Height: 6 m.
Minimum Spacing: 2 m.
Propagation: Semi-hardwood cuttings.
Comments: Foliage comes down near ground level.

Banksia ericifolia (Heath Banksia)
Height: 5 m.
Minimum Spacing: 1.5 m.
Propagation: Seed or semi-hardwood cuttings.
Comments: Dense, small-leafed screen. The hybrid 'Giant Candles' is a registered cultivar with long flower spikes.

Buckinghamia celsissima (Ivory Curl Flower)
Height: 3–5 m.
Minimum Spacing: 1.2 m.
Propagation: Seed or cuttings.
Comments: Thick foliage and excellent flower display. Light frosts only.

Callistemon salignus (Willow Bottlebrush)
Height: 6 m.
Minimum Spacing: 2 m.
Propagation: Seed or semi-hardwood cuttings.
Comments: Trim after flowering to promote new, pink growth. Light frosts only.

C. viminalis 'Hannah Ray' (Weeping Bottlebrush)
Height: 5 m.
Minimum Spacing: 2 m.
Propagation: Semi-hardwood cuttings.
Comments: Light screen. Trim off spent flowers.

Elaeocarpus reticulatus (Blueberry Ash)
Height: 5 m.
Minimum Spacing: 1.5 m.
Propagation: Semi-hardwood cuttings. Seed.
Comments: Needs ample water and freedom from heavy frosts.

Geijera parviflora (Wilga)
Height: 6 m.
Minimum Spacing: 1.5 m.
Propagation: Semi-hardwood cuttings (with difficulty).
Comments: Very drought hardy once established.

Melaleuca armillaris (Bracelet Honey Myrtle)
Height: 5 m.
Minimum Spacing: 2 m.

Propagation : Seed or semi-hardwood cuttings.
Comments: Very hardy. Best if regularly trimmed.

Pittosporum phillyreoides (Butterbush)
Height: 5 m.
Minimum Spacing: 2 m.
Propagation: Seed.
Comments: Attractive, perfumed flowers. Very drought hardy once established. Good for inland.

P. rhombifolium (QLD Pittosporum)
Height: 8 m.
Minimum Spacing: 2 m.
Propagation: Seed. May take months to germinate.
Comments: Frost hardy once established.

P. undulatum (Native Daphne)
Height: 6 m.
Minimum Spacing: 2 m.
Propagation: Seed.
Comments: Free seeding into bushland. Very hardy but needs ample water for fast growth.

Syzygium leuhmannii (Riberry)
Height: 5 m.
Minimum Spacing: 2 m.
Propagation: Seed.
Comments: Wonderful screen. Needs ample water and no more than light frosts.

Waterhousia floribunda (Weeping Lilly Pilly)
Height: 10 m.
Minimum Spacing: 2 m.
Propagation: Seed.
Comments: Probably too big for suburban gardens, but great screen for parks and large properties.

Exotics
Arbutus unedo (Irish Strawberry)
Height: 5 m.
Minimum Spacing: 2 m.

Propagation: Seed.
Comments: Very cold hardy.

Azara lanceolata (**Lance-leafed Azara**)
Height: 5 m.
Minimum Spacing: 1.5 m.
Propagation: Seed. Semi-hardwood cuttings.
Comments: Best in some shade and in cooler climates.

Hoheria populnea (**NZ Lace Bark**)
Height: 5 m.
Minimum Spacing: 2 m.
Propagation: Semi-hardwood cuttings.
Comments: Cold hardy but needs ample water.

Photinia × *fraseri* '**Red Robin**', '**Robusta**' (**Photinia**)
See Medium Hedges and Screens p. 54.

Pittosporum eugenioides '**Variegatum**' (**Variegated Pittosporum**)
See Medium Hedges and Screens p. 54.

P. tenuifolium '**James Stirling**' (**James Stirling Pittosporum**)
Height: 4 m.
Minimum Spacing: 1.2 m.
Propagation: Semi-hardwood cuttings.
Comments: Dainty, fast-growing screen for wide climate range.

Conifers For Large Screens
Chamaecyparis obtusa '**Crippsii**' (**Cripp's Golden Cypress**)
Height: 4 m.
Minimum Spacing: 1.5 m.
Propagation: Semi-hardwood cuttings taken in winter.
Comments: Slow growing. Must have sunny position.

x *Cupressocyparis leylandii* (**Leyland Cypress**)
See Medium Hedges and Screens p. 55.

Cupressus torulosa (**Bhutan Cypress**)
See Medium Hedges and Screens p. 55.

Juniperus chinensis '**Keteleeri**' (**Keteleer Juniper**)

Height: 5 m.
Minimum Spacing: 1.2 m.
Propagation: Semi-hardwood cuttings taken in winter.
Comments: Wide climate range. Slow growth.

Podocarpus elatus (**Illawarra Plum**)
P. falcatus (**Plum Pine**)
See Medium Hedges and Screens p. 56.

Thuja plicata '**Zebrina**' (**Western Red Cedar**)
Height: 4 m.
Minimum Spacing: 1.2 m.
Propagation: Semi-hardwood cuttings taken in winter.
Comments: Hardy conifer. Slow growing.

Windbreaks

Windbreaks are used to protect gardens and properties and to reduce the force of the wind. They are most often seen in exposed country areas or in coastal situations (*see* Seaside Shelter p. 81). In suburban situations the presence of other houses and gardens gives some protection from strong breezes, and wind is usually only a problem in hilltop sites. Here there is often a view to be preserved and sometimes it is necessary to weigh up the benefits of wind protection against any loss of that outlook.

Wind protection is directly related to the height of the windbreak. A good windbreak will reduce the force of the wind by between ten and 20 times the height of the plants used. The most effective protection is given when plants are placed in rows of ascending height, but even a single line of trees will provide some form of defence. Windbreak plants should have a good branching structure that offers at least 60 per cent cover and must have hard, preferably small, leaves that are not easily damaged.

Sometimes the best windbreaks are formed by mixed plantings with variations of height and, if space permits, some grouping of plants so that they do not form a regimented line. The frontline of a windbreak can be staggered so that it does not meet the wind's force head on. There is, however, a dramatic effect produced by a strong, single line of plants that can look very impressive in a bleak, windswept location.

When planting windbreaks, try, if at all possible, to avoid the use of stakes. Recent research has shown that staking interferes with the plant's natural development and may actually produce a plant that is weaker and less flexible. If staking is absolutely necessary, then use at least three stakes and loosely tie the plant between them using a 'figure-of-eight' tie. This will allow the plant some natural movement. Very small plants may need hessian or plastic sleeves around them to offer initial protection, but make sure that young trees surrounded by plastic do not 'cook' in the summer sun.

The best place to go for local guidance when choosing windbreak trees is a plant nursery run by one of the state forestry departments. Not only do these nurseries sell suitable plants, but they have access to detailed references and lots of good advice based on first-hand experience.

Natives

Surprisingly, we can look to the rainforest for some trees that are strong enough to serve in windbreaks. The real 'toughies' in the rainforest plants are the silky oak (*Grevillea robusta*) and two plants that were once in the same genus but have now been separated — water gum (*Tristaniopsis laurina*) and brush box (*Lophostemon confertus* syn. *Tristania conferta*). They are remarkably cold hardy and, once established, drought tolerant although the water gum, as its name indicates, is much happier with a regular supply of moisture. These three trees develop high canopies as they age so are more suitable as components of a windbreak rather than a screen. There is a variegated leaf form of the brush box that is smaller growing and develops delightful pink bark. It must be grafted, with difficulty, onto a seedling rootstock and this makes it very expensive to buy.

The turpentine (*Syncarpia glomulifera*) is from the rainforest borders where it grows slowly to 12 – 20 metres high. Its timber is so hard and decay resistant that it was originally used for bridge and wharf supports that were placed directly into salt water. It makes an excellent windbreak in substantially frost-free areas and grows to about ten metres.

Many of the eucalypts have been employed over the years as windbreaks. Not every eucalypt is suitable, as there are more than 500 species to choose from and they range from tiny shrubs to the world's tallest hardwood, the mountain ash (*Eucalyptus regnans*). One of the most popular for a windbreak is the tallowwood (*E. microcorys*) which has the desirable quality of maintaining bushiness low down on the trunk. This bushiness can be increased if the tree is pruned in its early stages of growth. Tallowwood has a thick fibrous bark which develops interesting furrows as the tree ages.

Unfortunately, tallowwood is only suitable for warm areas and other species should be selected for frosty climates. Tasmanian blue gum (*E. globulus*) is much more cold hardy and has been planted extensively in Canberra as a protective screen. It is one of the world's most beautiful trees with triangular, blue juvenile leaves; amazingly long, dark green adult leaves; and strange, warty fruit. It is extremely fast growing but does need plenty of room. There is a more compact form which can sometimes be obtained and will grow to about half the full size.

Bangalay (*E. botryoides*) is another big grower that can handle moderate frosts and is also able to cope with saline soils. However, if space is a problem look for the dwarf sugar gum (*E. cladocalyx* 'Nana'). 'Dwarf' in this instance is a relative term as this tree will still grow to around seven metres, but it is thick and bushy and stands up well to wind, cold and drought. Even when grown from seed, it retains its dwarf habit; just make sure the seed is from a reliable source.

Some of the best windbreak trees are the native she-oaks, or casuarinas. Strangely, these are often more appreciated overseas than in their homeland. They have been used extensively in New Zealand to protect orchards and in the Sahara desert to stabilise sand dunes. They are native to many of the warmer parts of the world and I have even seen them in Hawaii as a low, clipped, formal hedge. Many species are available (some now classed as *Allocasuarina* species) but one of the most versatile is the swamp oak (*Casuarina glauca*) which will grow almost anywhere, even where there is brackish water. Other desirable she-oaks are the river oak (*C. cunninghamiana*) and the forest oak (*Allocasuarina torulosa*). Desert oak (*A. decaisneana*) is particularly drought tolerant and is suitable for the driest inland areas while some other species will grow where they are exposed to salt spray.

Casuarinas avoid water loss by reducing their leaves to tiny scales, which gives them the appearance of conifer-like needles. They make a characteristic and pleasant 'swishing' sound when they move in the wind. Casuarinas have some ability to fix atmospheric nitrogen, which means that they can survive without supplementary fertilising.

The native cypress pines belong to the genus *Callitris* and some of these make good windbreaks. White cypress (*C. hugelii*) is sometimes called *C. glauca*, which is a reference to its glaucous, grey-green foliage. In its native habitat it grows in a pyramid or dome shape to about 15 metres and is hardy to inland conditions. The black cypress (*C. endlicheri*) will grow in similar conditions but is not as attractive as white cypress. Other cypress pines such as *C. columellaris*, or the smaller growing *C. rhomboidea* (Port Jackson cypress) have very upright, formal habits and are useful as a narrow screen. All these native cypress pines need good drainage and many of them, like some bottlebrush, hold onto their cones for years until they are forced by the heat of a bushfire to open and release their seeds.

Two of the paperbarks are useful components in a windbreak and will fill in well under some of the taller growing trees. *Melaleuca linariifolia* is called snow in summer, because of the way in which the white flowers sit on top of the branches like an out of season snowfall. The prickly paper bark (*M. styphelioides*) has sharp points on its leaves and cream, brush-like flowers in spring and summer. Both species will tolerate some salt air, occasional waterlogging, moderate frosts and a wide range of soils.

Exotics

When trees from other parts of the world are used as windbreaks, it is important to find out as much as possible about their natural growing conditions so that you can reproduce these conditions as closely as possible. Remember that Australia is the world's driest continent and this means that it is likely that exotic trees will need some supplementary watering when they are young. Even when well established, they will probably have to be helped through dry periods. As well, Australian soils are very poor and introduced trees will need fertilising to compensate for this deficiency. Too often this is done enthusiastically when the trees are young but, as they age, they are left to their own devices. If anything, fertilising is more important later in the tree's life as by then the roots have used up the goodness in the surrounding soil.

Introduced trees that are used as windbreaks must have hard leaves that can survive the battering of wind gusts without suffering too much damage. As a general rule, deciduous trees are not widely used because their branches are leafless for almost half the year and because their soft, new leaves are most vulnerable in early spring, which is often the windiest season. However in cold, dry areas, successful windbreaks have been established using the desert ash (*Fraxinus oxycarpa*) or the Australian-raised cultivar, claret ash (*F. oxycarpa* 'Raywoodii') which colours a beautiful wine red in autumn. Interestingly, the name *Fraxinus* comes from the Greek word *fraxis* which means 'to divide' and refers to the use of the tree in ancient times to mark boundaries and divisions of property. These ashes usually grow to about ten metres.

The pin oak (*Quercus palustris*) is another deciduous tree that makes a good windbreak in cool areas with a plentiful supply of water. *Palustris* means 'swamp-loving' and these trees are happy in spots with clay soil or bouts of poor drainage. The leaves colour a beautiful rich crimson in autumn before turning brown. They hang on the tree all through winter until pushed off by the new shoots in spring. This ability to hold on to the old leaves means that the tree continues to give protection right through the cold weather. By oak standards, pin oak is reasonably fast growing.

The peppercorn tree (*Schinus areira*) seems to survive in very harsh, inland areas and, once established, can stand up to periods of drought. Peppercorns are beautiful trees with fine, evergreen leaves and drooping branches. They must have good drainage and seem to prefer growing in poor, stony ground but they are best in areas that stay above − 3°C.

Peppercorns flower in summer with clusters of small, white flowers and these are followed, on female trees, by bunches of bright, pink berries. These are not used to make the pepper of commerce but can be dried and stored until spring when they can be sown in seed-raising mix to produce a crop of new trees.

Peppercorns make ideal windbreaks because they are so hardy and because, although they grow between eight and ten metres tall, they branch from within a couple of metres of the ground. They are very long-lived and old trees develop gnarled and twisted trunks that become increasingly attractive with age.

Conifers

Some of the larger growing introduced conifers have been widely planted as windbreaks. Surely the most common must be the monterey pine (*Pinus radiata*) which makes up more than 60 per cent of commercial tree plantations in Australia. These pines grow to a bigger size (potentially 20 metres high) in Australia than they do in their native California. In subtropical climates they can be replaced by the slash pine (*P. elliottii*) or the Mexican pine (*P. patula*), and in the hot dry inland by the smaller growing aleppo pine (*P. halepensis*).

Another Californian conifer has also been widely used as a windbreak on country properties. This is the golden form of the lambert cypress (*Cupressus macrocarpa* 'Lambertiana-aurea') which has strong, spreading horizontal branches that grow right down to the ground. This plant must be propagated from cuttings so that the golden colouring will be reproduced. It is most suited to cold areas with good rainfall but low humidity and in a happy spot will eventually reach a height of more than 10 metres. It has fallen from favour in recent years as it has been found to be susceptible to the fungal disease, cypress canker.

From India comes the versatile deodar cedar (*Cedrus deodara*) which is a very hardy plant with sweeping branches and grey-green foliage. It develops in a natural windbreak shape with a very wide base that gradually tapers to a conical peak with a nodding tip. The squat, glaucous cones sit on top of the branches like Christmas decorations.

Deodar cedar grows in a wide range of climates but in dry districts will need some supplementary watering. It will reach between ten and 15 metres depending on soil type and the base will spread across five to seven metres. If money is no object, these trees successfully transplant when quite large so you can use them to create an instant screen.

All these conifers should only be trimmed on the young, outer edges because they will not reshoot from older wood. Because they have needles, rather than leaves, they are well equipped to stand up to strong winds and help break their force.

Checklist: Windbreak Trees

Natives
Allocasuarina decaisneana (**Desert Oak**)
Height: 10 m.
Minimum Spacing: 3 m.
Propagation: Seed.
Comments: Useful for hot, dry inland.

A. torulosa (**Forest Oak**)
Height: 10 m.
Minimum Spacing: 3 m.
Propagation: Seed.
Comments: Hardy and attractive in most areas.

Casuarina cunninghamiana (**River Oak**)
Height: 10 m.

Minimum Spacing: 3 m.
Propagation: Seed.
Comments: Attractive she-oak for a wide range of conditions.

C. glauca (Swamp Oak)
Height: 10 m.
Minimum Spacing: 3 m.
Propagation: Seed.
Comments: More rounded outline than the river oak but equally adaptable to a wide range of conditions.

Eucalyptus botryoides (Bangalay)
Height: 15 m.
Minimum Spacing: 4 m.
Propagation: Seed.
Comments: Frost hardy and useful for salty soils.

E. cladocalyx 'Nana' (Dwarf Sugar Gum)
Height: 7 m.
Minimum Spacing: 2 m.
Propagation: Seed.
Comments: Very adaptable tree.

E. globulus (Tasmanian Blue Gum)
Height: 20 m.
Minimum Spacing: 4 m.
Propagation: Seed.
Comments: Fast-growing, cold hardy, big and beautiful.

E. microcorys (Tallowwood)
Height: 20 m.
Minimum Spacing: 3 m.
Propagation: Seed.
Comments: Frost tender. Low branching but benefits from pruning to thicken tree when young.

Grevillea robusta (Silky Oak)
Height: 10 m.
Minimum Spacing: 3 m.
Propagation: Seed.
Comments: Upright growth. Beautiful yellow flowers in early summer. Will grow in most areas.

Lophostemon confertus (Brush Box)

Height: 10 m.

Minimum Spacing: 3 m.

Propagation: Seed.

Comments: Hardy and much planted tree. A form with variegated leaves is available.

Melaleuca linariifolia (Snow in Summer)

Height: 7 m.

Minimum Spacing: 2 m.

Propagation: Seed.

Comments: Hardy and adaptable if given ample water. Good for clay soils.

M. styphelioides (Prickly Paper Bark)

Height: 7 m.

Minimum Spacing: 2 m.

Propagation: Seed.

Comments: Will grow almost anywhere, including saline soils.

Syncarpia glomulifera (Turpentine)

Height: 12 m.

Minimum Spacing: 3 m.

Propagation: Seed.

Comments: Slow growing. Will only take light frosts.

Tristaniopsis laurina (Water Gum)

Height: 6 m.

Minimum Spacing: 2 m.

Propagation: Seed.

Comments: Hardy to drought, excess moisture and moderate frosts. Clusters of yellow, summer flowers.

Exotic Trees
Fraxinus oxycarpa (Desert Ash)
F. oxycarpa 'Raywoodii' (Claret Ash)

Height: 10 m.

Minimum Spacing: 4 m.

Propagation: Species grown from seed. Cultivar grafted onto a seedling understock.

Comments: Deciduous tree which, once established, can survive in hot, dry districts.

Quercus palustris (**Pin Oak**)
Height: 10 m.
Minimum Spacing: 4 m.
Propagation: Seed.
Comments: Deciduous tree that holds on to its brown leaves during winter. Tolerates damp soil and must have good water supply.

Schinus areira (**Peppercorn**)
Height: 10 m.
Minimum Spacing: 4 m.
Propagation: Seed.
Comments: Very drought resistant and hardy. Branches close to ground. 'Peppercorns' only occur on female trees.

Conifers
Callitris endlicheri (**Black Cypress**)
C. hugelii (**White Cypress**)
Height: 8 m.
Minimum Spacing: 1.5 m.
Propagation: Seed.
Comments: Fast growing native conifers with upright growth that can become more spreading in old age and in colder climates. Useful for sandy soils.

Cedrus deodara (**Deodar Cedar**)
Height: 10 m.
Minimum Spacing: 3 m.
Propagation: Seed.
Comments: Pyramidal shape with blue-grey foliage. Grows in wide climatic range.

Cupressus macrocarpa '**Lambertiana Aurea**' (**Golden Lambert Cypress**)
Height: 8 m.
Minimum Spacing: 3 m.
Propagation: Semi-hardwood cuttings. (Difficult.)
Comments: Creates a majestic, sweeping windbreak for large properties. Trim only on young growth. Susceptible to cypress canker.

Pinus elliottii (**Slash Pine**)
Height: 10 m.
Minimum Spacing: 3 m.

Propagation: Seed.
Comments: Useful large windbreak tree for warm coastal areas.

P. halepensis (Aleppo Pine)
Height: 10 m.
Minimum Spacing: 3 m.
Propagation: Seed.
Comments: Useful windbreak tree for hot, dry areas.

P. patula (Mexican Pine)
Height: 10 m.
Minimum Spacing: 3 m.
Propagation: Seed.
Comments: Attractive, drooping needles. Good tree for warm areas.

P. radiata (Monterey Pine)
Height: 15 m.
Minimum Spacing: 4 m.
Propagation: Seed.
Comments: Adapts to almost all conditions.

A screen of cumquats.

Chilean willow will do well in that difficult damp spot.

Purple hop bush: a 'tall and skinny'.

Bhutan cypress.

Lantana, once used for hedging, is now a serious bushland pest.

Seaside Shelter

If you garden in a windswept coastal location then you have two major problems to contend with. First, there is the constant battering of the salt-laden winds that can burn the leaves of tender plants, and secondly, the soil you are working with will be sandy and poor and will have difficulty in holding water and nutrients. Your aim in a seaside garden will be not so much to provide privacy from onlookers, but protection from the unrelenting onslaught of the elements.

Start by looking at what nature has done in similar situations. She starts by germinating small, ground-hugging plants that bind the soil together, then allows taller plants to spring up among these ground covers. You can hasten this process by building a non-living screen of wire mesh, wooden lattice or tea tree poles which will protect your new plants. At the same time, use organic matter to improve the quality of your soil. It is best not to build a solid screen such as a brick wall as this contributes to the turbulent effect of the sea winds; a 60:40 ratio of solid screen to openings seems to be ideal. The non-living screen may be just a temporary affair that is there to help get your plantings established.

When choosing plant material, begin by selecting the tallest-growing and toughest plants for the ocean side. That way, these tall shrubs and trees will help protect the more vulnerable smaller plants within the garden. In exposed positions the wind usually has a pruning and stunting effect on the frontline plants and they grow to lesser heights than would be expected in a more sheltered situation, so look around at the same plants growing in your immediate neighbourhood for guidance as to ultimate size.

When planting, dig old organic matter or compost into the soil and mulch well to avoid leaching of the nutrients. In some very open positions, the wind can actually blow the soil surface away and in this case it might be best to use a strong mulch such as woven mulchmat, chicken wire, or stones and gravel. These can be removed after the plants are established.

Once your shelter is well grown and your garden protected, then you can experiment with other, more delicate, plantings. But be realistic and weigh up the advantages and disadvantages of your seaside location. Don't expect to grow cool climate, highland plants right on the coast; if you must have an English-style garden full of deciduous shrubs and soft perennials, then sell up and move to the mountains!

Front Line Plantings

A mixed row of taller plantings will look attractive and take advantage of the best features of individual shrubs, but if you wish a more uniform look then you can plant a row of a single species. Coastal strips from around the world have provided us with a selection of screening plants from which to choose.

If you live on the east coast of Australia then you will almost certainly have seen stands of the coast banksia (*Banksia integrifolia*) which flourish defiantly in the full blast of salt winds. The leaves on young plants are distinctly toothed but become smooth-edged as the tree matures. They are dark green on top and have grey hairs on their under surface that help to protect the leaves from salt damage. Coast banksia has upright, pale yellow flower cones that appear near the branch ends all through the colder part of the year. The flowers are excellent for picking and are lightly perfumed. The ultimate height of *B. integrifolia* varies with conditions, but it usually reaches about eight metres.

The other native that also grows on sand dunes and in the teeth of gales is the horsetail oak (*Casuarina equisetifolia* var. *incana*) with slightly open growth (which can be thickened by pruning) and very long, needle-like leaf stems. It has a very weeping habit and the thick bunches of drooping leaves do look like slightly unkempt horsetails. Another she-oak which can handle frontline coastal conditions, *Allocasuarina verticillata*, is still most commonly known by its old name of *Casuarina stricta*. It too has weeping growth and is often called the drooping she-oak. Both species are very effective soil binders and will usually grow to five metres.

The Sydney golden wattle (*Acacia longifolia*), with its bright yellow, rod-like flowers, has a form that grows right on the coast and is sometimes called *A. sophorae*. It is one of the first plants to move in onto sand dunes and it begins to hold the soil together so that other plants can follow on. This is known as 'plant succession' and when the wattle starts such a process it tends to stay as a very low shrub, but in more favourable conditions it can get up to five metres. Both the wattle and the she-oaks have the ability to convert their own nitrogen out of the air which helps them to establish on poor, sandy soils.

Norfolk Island hibiscus (*Lagunaria patersonia*) doesn't just grow on Norfolk Island but is also found naturally in Queensland. It is never far from the coast, however, and has grey-green leaves that use their hairy surfaces to protect themselves from salt spray. It has upright growth and is often planted two to three metres apart as a single species screen. It can eventually reach eight metres but stays branched well down the trunk so gives good shelter even when fully grown.

In spring and summer the Norfolk Island hibiscus is studded with single pink flowers that open to about six centimetres across. They are followed by the tree's major drawback — the brown seed pods that split open and release sharply-pointed, hairy splinters. This gives the tree another common name, the cow-itch tree, which was no doubt bestowed by the dairy farmers of Norfolk Island. Unfortunately, these hairs are also irritating to humans but they are not enough of a problem to dissuade you from planting this beautiful tree.

As well as the pretty pink blooms, Norfolk Island hibiscus is often decorated in the warmer weather by clusters of brightly coloured harlequin bugs. These brightly coloured bugs develop through many different stages, changing their jewel-like outer shells at each step along the way. Although they are sap-sucking insects, they don't appear to harm these trees and their brightly coloured presence is a bonus.

Norfolk Island hibiscus is not a true hibiscus but could be classed as a relative because it is in the same botanical family. However there is a hibiscus native to tropical coasts all over the world that can be used as part of a large, salt-resistant screen. This is the yellow-flowered *Hibiscus tiliaceus* which looks very delicate but uses the soft hairs on its leaves to protect it from salt. The single flowers turn a pinky-red before falling, which gives this large shrub an attractive, multi-coloured effect.

One of the best and most salt resistant plants for the coastline is New Zealand Christmas bush (*Metrosideros excelsa*). Its red, staminate flowers are most abundant at Christmas time but can also appear at other times of the year. The plant's roots are so tenacious that they will happily grow in salty sand and will cling to windswept cliffs. If the root system is buried by shifting sands, more roots will sprout further up the trunk.

New Zealand Christmas bush is also known by the Maori name 'Pohutukawa' which, fittingly, means 'drenched with salt spray'. It makes a solid screen to about five metres but its commonly available variegated form usually only gets to three metres. Regular trimming will keep lots of new growth on the outside of the plant.

Any of these tall shrubs can be used as a first line of defence against salt winds. They will establish more readily if given some protection when first planted and if helped with regular watering and mulching.

Second Line Plantings

Second line plants do not have to be as hardy as those in the first line but they play an important part in giving depth and strength to the coastal screen.

New Zealand mirror plant (*Coprosma repens*) is tough enough to grow in the front line facing the ocean but, as it seldom reaches two metres in height, it is a little short to give protection to other plants. Its common name refers to the extremely shiny leaf surfaces, and it is this shiny coating that stops the leaves from absorbing the damaging salt. Mirror plants are most often seen in their variegated forms and are desirable foliage plants for almost any garden. They are best if regularly clipped to keep the new growth coming.

A similar shiny surface protects the leaves of the Japanese pittosporum (*Pittosporum tobira*) when it is used in a seaside garden. This shrub grows slowly to about three metres and has bunches of creamy-white, perfumed flowers in spring and summer. It is drought resistant and should be planted more often as it is both tough and good looking. Japanese pittosporum does not appreciate being trimmed, so place it where it can eventually reach its full height.

Some of the conifers are hardy enough to be grown in a coastal screen. Of course, the hardiest of all is the Norfolk Island pine (*Araucaria heterophylla*), but it grows too large and is too open to be function as a screen plant. Still, there are some others that would make useful punctuation marks in a second line coastal defence. The best native conifer is the Port Jackson cypress (*Callitris rhomboidea*) which has evolved on poor sandstone soils like those that occur in rock pockets in the coastal suburbs of Sydney. Its ultimate height depends on soil depth and can range from six to ten metres. It is characterised by the drooping ends on the new branches. Port Jackson cypress trims readily and the columnar growth would suit quite formal gardens.

The leyland cypress (× *Cupressocyparis leylandii*), too, will cope with some salt exposure if it is given a little bit of protection from the full blast of the sea breeze. This is because one of its parents, the nootka cypress, is found growing naturally on the Alaskan coastline. Like the Port Jackson cypress, leyland cypress can be used to produce a formal effect but would need to be hedged to prevent it from growing up into the full force of the salt-laden winds.

Even though your seaside shelter performs such an important function, this does not mean that you are unable to include some pretty flowering shrubs. Try using the white Indian hawthorn (*Raphiolepis indica*) or its pink blooming hybrid, *R.* × *delacourii*. Any of the hebes, too, can cope with some exposure and display blooms in shades of pink, white, purple or blue. There are even some cultivars with variegated leaves which will add to foliage interest.

Probably the best flowering shrub for a coastal position is the much maligned oleander. Oleanders (*Nerium oleander*) grow so easily that we tend to take them for granted and they become totally neglected. No plant can look at its best if it is given no care but, if regularly trimmed and fertilised, oleander will reward you with a summer long display of showy blooms. I once travelled from the east coast of the US to the west and was amazed to find it was oleanders growing along the Californian highway that were causing my fellow bus passengers from New York to exclaim with delight. Like most people who grew up with oleanders, I tended to regard them as weeds, but seeing them through someone else's eyes has given me new respect for these underrated plants.

They are also regarded with horror because they are poisonous, but so many plants in our gardens are poisonous that it's surprising that we single out this genus for disapproval. It is far safer to teach children not to eat the leaves or wood of any garden plant than to think that by refusing to grow oleanders we are solving the whole problem.

Oleanders flower in shades of red, pink, salmon and white, so can be used to create a colourful mixed screen. There is a related plant (also poisonous) called yellow oleander (*Thevetia peruviana*), which has bright golden blooms but needs subtropical conditions. The common oleanders are more cold hardy but will be damaged by heavy frosts. They can grow to three metres but look more attractive if trimmed to about two metres.

Most coastal gardeners dream despairingly about growing roses but there is one type of rose — *Rosa rugosa* — that will grow by the sea. *R. rugosa* is a Japanese species with rich green, deeply veined leaves and stems that are covered with fine thorns. Rugosa flowers are single or semi-double and come in pinks, purples and white. The main flowering is in spring but they can spot bloom through summer and autumn. After flowering, the bright orange or red rosehips develop and decorate the bush for months. Like most roses, rugosas lose their leaves in winter, which reduces their effectiveness as part of a protective screen.

Many Mediterranean plants have evolved on windswept coastal dunes and have been popular garden plants for centuries. Plants such as lavender and rosemary are equipped with hairs on their leaf surfaces that can handle salt. Lavender, rosemary and rock rose (*Cistus* species) all grow to about one metre and are hardy to sea breezes. They need good drainage so are happiest in sandy soil.

Lavender is best known for its fragrant flower spikes but rosemary and rock roses have become associated with soldiers and war. For rosemary, the connection goes right back to ancient Rome when a soldier would pick a sprig of rosemary on an Italian hillside and present it to his comrade as a token of loyalty and support for the forthcoming battle.

Rock rose has a far more recent and parochial association with battles — Australian soldiers in the first world war are said to have brought back rock roses from Gallipoli. (This sounds like a myth to me: I'm sure they had too many other things on their minds!) Whatever its history, rock rose is extremely hardy and has very pretty, crepey flowers that are similar to those of rugosa roses.

One native plant is so much like the European rosemary that it has been given the common name of coast rosemary. *Westringia fruticosa* is in the same botanical family as rosemary and has a herb-like aroma in its blue-grey leaves. It is tolerant of a wide range of soils and conditions and makes an excellent clipped, formal hedge. Like the true rosemary, the hairy leaf surfaces protect the foliage from salt damage. Westringia grows to about one and a half metres and flowers for much of the year with faintly mauve blooms that are partly hidden among the leaves.

Checklist: Seaside Shelter

Front Line Plantings
Acacia longifolia var. *sophorae* (**Sydney Golden Wattle**)
Height: 3 m.
Minimum Spacing: 1 m.
Propagation: Scarified seed. Pour over boiling water and allow to cool.
Comments: Height of plant varies according to conditions.

Allocasuarina verticillata (**Drooping She-oak**)
Height: 5 m.
Minimum Spacing: 3 m.
Propagation: Seed.
Comments: Fast growing.

Banksia integrifolia (**Coast Banksia**)
Height: 4 m.
Minimum Spacing: 1.2 m.
Propagation: Seed.
Comments: Very tolerant of salt spray.

Casuarina equisetifolia var. *incana* (**Horsetail Oak**)
Height: 5 m.
Minimum Spacing: 3 m.
Propagation: Seed.
Comments: Very pendulous outer branches with coarse 'needles'.

Hibiscus tiliaceus (**Yellow-flowered Hibiscus**)
Height: 5 m.
Minimum Spacing: 1.2 m.
Propagation: Seed or tip cuttings.
Comments: Must have full sun and be in frost-free area.

Lagunaria patersonia (**Norfolk Island Hibiscus**)
Height: 8 m.
Minimum Spacing: 2 m.
Propagation: Seed.
Comments: Hardy tree with delicate looking pink blooms.

Metrosideros excelsa (**NZ Christmas Bush**)
See Medium Hedges and Screens p. 53.

Second Line Plantings
Callitris rhomboidea (Port Jackson Cypress)
Height: 8 m.
Minimum Spacing: 1 m.
Propagation: Seed.
Comments: Very columnar and formal growth. Needs sandy, well-drained soil.

Cistus × *purpureus* 'Brilliancy' (Rock Rose)
Height: 1 m.
Minimum Spacing: 75 cm.
Propagation: Semi-hardwood cuttings.
Comments: Many different types of rock rose are available, all well worth growing. They need good drainage and sun. They dislike summer humidity.

Coprosma repens (Mirror Plant)
Height: 2 m.
Minimum Spacing: 1 m.
Propagation: Semi-hardwood cuttings. Ground layers.
Comments: Very salt resistant and pollution resistant.

× *Cupressocyparis leylandii* (Leyland Cypress)
See Medium Hedges and Screens p. 55.

Hebe speciosa 'La Seduisante' (Hebe Veronica)
Hebe cultivars
See Low Hedges and Screens p. 36.

Lavandula angustifolia (English Lavender)
L. dentata (French Lavender)
Height: 1 m.
Minimum Spacing: 50 cm.
Propagation: Semi-hardwood tip cuttings.
Comments: Both species need good drainage and full sun. Clip after flushes of flowers.

Nerium oleander (Oleander)
Height: 3 m.
Minimum Spacing: 1 m.
Propagation: Semi-hardwood cuttings.
Comments: Very hardy and free flowering. Colours range from white to pink and red. Prune lightly after flowering.

Pittosporum tobira (**Japanese Pittosporum**)
Height: 3 m.
Minimum Spacing: 1.5 m.
Propagation: Semi-hardwood cuttings. (Difficult).
Comments: Can be hard to find and does not like being cut back, but well worth growing as part of mixed screen.

Raphiolepis × *delacourii* (**Pink Indian Hawthorn**)
R. indica (**Indian Hawthorn**)
See Low Hedges and Screens p. 37.

Rosa rugosa (**Japanese Rose**)
Height: 1–2 m.
Minimum Spacing: 1 m.
Propagation: Hardwood cuttings.
Comments: Possibly the hardiest type of rose. Deciduous.

Rosmarinus officinalis (**Rosemary**)
Height: 1.5 m.
Minimum Spacing: 50 cm.
Propagation: Semi-hardwood tip cuttings.
Comments: Slow growing. Needs good drainage but adaptable to many climates.

Thevetia peruviana (**Yellow Oleander**)
Height: 2 m.
Minimum Spacing: 1 m.
Propagation: Seed or semi-hardwood cuttings.
Comments: Poisonous, so best to remove spent flowers before fruit forms. Frost-free climates.

Westringia fruticosa (**Coast Rosemary**)
See Low Hedges and Screens p. 41.

Special Purpose Hedges and Screens

Fragrant Hedges and Screens

A hedge or screen that has fragrant flowers or foliage can give great delight to a gardener and to visitors that come to the garden. This is especially so if fragrant plants are used to make a clipped hedge, because the very act of clipping is a pleasure when you are cutting into perfumed foliage or working amongst scented blooms. A front hedge that is perfumed will greet your guests in the most inviting way.

Murraya paniculata, the cosmetic bark bush or orange jessamine, makes an attractive formal hedge or informal screen to about three metres. The clusters of white, orange-blossom-like flowers have a sweet perfume and clipping seems to encourage these flowers to display themselves on the outside of the bush.

There is a closely related native murraya, *M. ovatifolia*, that is a rainforest understorey plant in tropical Australia. Unfortunately, it can be hard to obtain but other scented natives are readily available in cultivation. The long-leafed waxflower (*Eriostemon myoporoides*) is a tolerant small shrub with winter flowers that are starry and white. These have a herb-like perfume that is quite pleasant, especially when picked.

Other natives have scented oils in their leaves that protect them from pests and predators. Lemon-scented tea tree (*Leptospermum petersonii*) can be used unclipped as part of a tall screen or can be pruned to much less. The leaves need to be crushed or cut to release their lemon scent and this makes the job of pruning them very pleasant. The common name of the lemon-scented tea tree is not misleading; the leaves can be infused in hot water to make a refreshing, hot lemon drink.

I have not heard of anyone making tea from the leaves of lemon-scented myrtles (*Backhousia citriodora*) but they are in the same botanical family as the tea tree. Lemon-scented myrtle grows as an upright tree and is not usually hedged in the manner of the tea tree but you can get a lemon 'charge' out of crushing the leaves and, at the same time, enjoy the faint honey fragrance of the spring and summer flowers.

The native frangipani (*Hymenosporum flavum*) also grows in an upright manner but can get to ten metres in favourable conditions. It is a beautiful fence plant that has scented white, trumpet-shaped flowers that age to a creamy-yellow. It needs to be in warm conditions, so appreciates the company of other plants.

All of the pittosporums seem to have flowers with some sort of perfume and native daphne (*Pittosporum undulatum*) is no exception. Its spring blooms are particularly heavily scented at night because the tree uses this scent to attract the night flying moths that are its pollinators. It will only grow in fairly warm areas with good rainfall but in the dry inland its close relative the butterbush (*P. phillyreoides*) will flourish, and flower in scented profusion in winter and spring.

Japanese pittosporum (*P. tobira*), which is so useful in a seaside screen, grows to large shrub size and has clusters of scented white blooms. The New Zealand cousins (*P. eugenioides* 'Variegatum' and *P. tenuifolium*) are much less inclined to show off and their flowers are often hidden by the foliage. *P. eugenioides* has pale yellow flowers that are well-camouflaged among the variegated leaves, while the flowers of *P. tenuifolium* cultivars are purplish-brown, aging to near black. Both species, however, give out a strong perfume that is particularly noticeable at night.

Osmanthus heterophyllus, from Japan, has leaves that are so holly-like that one could be forgiven for assuming that this upright, spiky shrub was a holly. If you're not sure, look at the leaf arrangement; osmanthus leaves, unlike those of holly, are always arranged in opposite pairs. Osmanthus blooms, although small, are strongly perfumed and are followed by blue berries. The plant's spiny leaves help make this a useful barrier shrub that can be grown in place of a fence. There is another Japanese osmanthus, *O. fragrans*, with even more strongly scented, tiny flowers, but it needs to be constantly pruned to make it grow thickly enough for a hedge. Both osmanthus species will grow in a wide range of climates but look at their best in semi-shade.

Some people love the perfume of port wine magnolia (*Michelia figo*) and others find it too strong to bear. It's certainly a 'fruity' fragrance which is borne out by its other common name — banana shrub. It is closely related to magnolias and its purple and yellow flowers do look like miniature, strangely-coloured magnolia blossoms. It tends to be slow growing but eventually makes a bulky, dense shrub to about three metres with handsome, glossy foliage. It's probably best used as part of a mixed, informal screen.

The flowers of port wine magnolia are usually well hidden among the leaves and, if it wasn't for the perfume, we wouldn't even notice that they were there. Neither would the pollinating insects, which is why these plants with insignificant or white flowers use fragrance to attract attention. The same is true of the lance-leaf azara (*Azara lanceolata*). This upright shrub with small toothed leaves has greeny-yellow, fluffy blooms that have a distinctly vanilla aroma. You can't produce your own vanilla from this plant, however: true vanilla comes from the seed pod of a tree-dwelling orchid!

Edible Hedges and Screens

Edible hedges and screens serve a double purpose. Not only can you benefit from their screening properties, but you are able to enjoy their produce. What could be nicer than giving a jar of your own brandied cumquats as a personal Christmas gift? Cumquats are most often seen as decorative pot plants but their other landscaping possibilities should not be overlooked. They are excellent screening plants and have close, twiggy growth that clips well, so can be used as part of a formal hedge.

The toughest and easiest to grow seems to be the calamondin, which is thought to be a cross between a true cumquat and a mandarin. It grows to between two and three metres and flowers in late spring. The small, round fruit that develop in autumn hang on to the bush all through winter. They look like little oranges but are very bitter to eat and are usually preserved in liqueur or made into marmalade.

True cumquats (*Fortunella* species) have much more palatable fruit that can be eaten straight off the tree. Their skin is very sweet and makes a pleasant contrast with the slightly sour flesh. Cumquats fruit later than calamondins and the fruit doesn't seem to hang on to the tree for quite as long, but that may be because it tastes so good it gets eaten very quickly. Cumquats, like all citrus, need good drainage but are more cold tolerant than lemons or oranges.

One variety, called the 'teardrop cumquat', has oval fruit while the other popular variety bears fruit that are similar in shape to those of the calamondin. Both types come from China and are considered by the Chinese to bring good luck. If one plant in a pot is considered lucky, think how much good fortune would flow from a whole hedge!

Other fruit trees can be used as part of a screen. Olives have been cultivated for thousands of years and some individual plants are thought to be more than 2,000 years old. The plants are very hardy and will grow right on the coastline but are usually happier in inland conditions with less humidity. The leaves are protected by a layer of fine grey hairs which gives the tree a silvery appearance. Olive fruit can be picked, and pickled, when green, or left until it turns black.

Like the olive, feijoas have a hairy covering on their leaves, although mostly on the underside. They are sensitive to salt, however, and cannot be grown where there are sea breezes or brackish water. They are not quite as cold hardy as the olive but seem to be as tough in most other respects. Feijoa, or pineapple guava (*Feijoa sellowiana*), is a bushy decorative shrub that grows to about three metres and has very pretty red flowers in spring. These flowers have showy stamens in the centre and a skirt-like outer row of silver-grey bracts. They look like brightly coloured fuchsia blooms.

Feijoas usually need more than one plant for cross-pollination to develop fruit, so planting them as a hedge should maximise your cropping. The fruit does not ripen on the bush but must be picked when mature and left to soften. You can tell when a fruit is mature because it will pull easily from the tree.

Another guava, the cherry guava (*Psidium littorale*), is undervalued as a landscaping plant. It usually grows to a three metre, bushy shrub although it can reach five metres and develop a tree-like trunk in old age. It has shiny, evergreen leaves and white staminate flowers in spring. These are followed by red, cherry-sized autumn fruits that look like miniature pomegranates. The fruit has an acidic flavour and is most often used for jams and jellies, but I think that these shrubs are so tough and attractive, they should be grown just for their ornamental value, even if it means leaving the fruits for the birds. Although often listed as a tropical plant, cherry guava will tolerate moderately heavy frosts.

The Hawaiians would have us believe otherwise, but Australia is the home of the delicious macadamia nut. Macadamias are rainforest trees that can grow to 20 metres in their natural habitat but are most often seen in gardens as an upright, leafy tree to about five metres. One species, *Macadamia integrifolia*, has leaves in whorls of three, while in another, *M. tetraphylla*, the leaves come in fours. Both have attractive sprays of flowers in spring — white in *M. integrifolia* and pink in *M. tetraphylla*. Sometimes these flower spikes exhibit the rainforest characteristic 'cauliflory', growing directly out from the bare branches.

For guaranteed fruiting, it would be best to buy grafted macadamia plants but if you are basically using your plant as a screen then a seedling will do the job. Fruit size and quantity will then be a matter of genetic chance. Macadamias will only handle very light frosts and must be given plenty of water.

The last plant in this section is most often listed as a herb but is actually a woody shrub that grows to about four metres. This is the bay tree (*Laurus nobilis*) whose aromatic leaves are used in cooking. Bay trees have been cultivated since the time of the ancient Greeks when to be crowned with a laurel wreath was the highest accolade that could be awarded to an athlete or warrior.

Bay trees are very hardy and will grow in a wide climatic range. They respond well to clipping and can be trained into formal shapes. Female trees bear greeny-yellow flowers and black berries whose oil is used in the manufacture of perfume.

Hedges and Screens for Damp Spots

If you are planting a screen in a part of the garden that is constantly wet, your choice of plants will be very limited. One possibility is the Chilean, or pencil, willow that grows in a very upright narrow column. Like most willows, it doesn't mind constant damp around its roots and it must have a good water supply in order to stay well-leafed. The catch is that, if dry, it will send out roots looking for water and this can cause problems with sewerage and drainage pipes. Try to plant the trees at least five metres from such pipes, especially if they are more than ten years old, and keep the trees well watered in dry periods. Although classed as an evergreen, pencil willow becomes very thin in a cold winter.

The same is true of the evergreen alder (*Alnus jorullensis*), a fast-growing tree from Central America. Most alders grow as streamside plants with high water requirements and this tree is no exception. It forms an upright, cone shape to about ten metres with branches coming right down to the ground. It makes an excellent large screen for moist areas with enough room to accommodate its ultimate size. Like the pencil willow, it will tolerate light frosts but can lose some leaves in the colder part of the year.

Evergreen alder has toothed leaves on drooping branches, and fruit that develop like little woody cones. It is in the same family as silver birches and has some of the grace of that well-known group of plants.

As you would guess from its common name, the swamp oak (*Casuarina glauca*) can handle moist soil, even if that soil sometimes contains salt. *C. glauca* grows to at least ten metres and is very good for draining a damp area. It is so versatile that, once established, it can even handle dry periods. These tough qualities are shared by the swamp melaleuca (*Melaleuca quinquenervia*), an upright paperbark that grows naturally in coastal swamps. It has thick, spongy bark and lance-shaped leaves. It is often planted to stabilise sandy soils near the coast but is not tolerant to inland cold. If unpruned it will grow to ten metres but can be constantly cut back to keep it to a manageable size.

Checklist: Special Purpose Hedges and Screens

Fragrant Hedges and Screens
Azara lanceolata (**Lance-leafed Azara**)
See Tall Screens p. 69.

Backhousia citriodora (**Lemon-scented Myrtle**)
See Tall Screens p. 66.

Eriostemon myoporoides (**Long-leafed Waxflower**)
See Low Hedges and Screens p. 40.

Hymenosporum flavum (**Native Frangipani**)
Height: 10 m.
Minimum Spacing: 2 m.
Propagation: Seed.
Comments: Very light screen for frost-free districts.

Leptospermum petersonii (**Lemon-scented Tea Tree**)
See Medium Hedges and Screens p. 57.

Michelia figo (**Port Wine Magnolia**)
Height: 3 m.
Minimum Spacing: 1 m.
Propagation: Semi-hardwood cuttings.
Comments: Slow growing, dense screen. Will only take light frosts.

Murraya paniculata (**Orange Jessamine**)
M. ovatifolia (**Native Murraya**)
See Medium Hedges and Screens p. 54.

Osmanthus fragrans (**Sweet Osmanthus**)
O. heterophyllus (**Holly-leafed Osmanthus**)
Height: 3 m.
Minimum Spacing: 1 m.
Propagation: Semi-hardwood cuttings.
Comments: Slow growing but will tolerate a wide range of climates. Trim after flowering to maintain bushiness.

Pittosporum eugenioides 'Variegatum' (**Variegated Pittosporum**)
See Medium Hedges and Screens p. 54.

P. phillyreoides (**Butterbush**)
See Tall Screens p. 68.

P. tenuifolium cultivars (**NZ Pittosporum**)
Height: 1–4 m.
Minimum Spacing: 20 cm – 1.2 m.
Propagation: Semi-hardwood cuttings.
Comments: Range of foliage plants with insignificant, perfumed flowers. Hardy in a wide range of climates.

P. tobira (**Japanese Pittosporum**)
See Seaside Shelter p. 89.

P. undulatum (**Native Daphne**)
See Tall Screens p. 68.

Edible Hedges and Screens
Fortunella × *calamondin* (**Cumquat**)
F. margarita
Height: 3 m.
Cut to: 1 m.
Minimum Spacing: 75 cm.
Propagation: Usually budded onto seedling rootstock.
Comments: More cold hardy than other citrus. Need a sunny well-drained position.

Feijoa sellowiana (**Pineapple Guava**)
Height: 3 m.

Cut to: 1.5 m.
Minimum Spacing: 1 m.
Propagation: Seed.
Comments: Needs sunny, well-drained position. Safe to -2°C. Seedlings will only fruit if other plants are nearby for cross pollination.

Laurus nobilis (Bay Tree)
Height: 4 m.
Cut to: 1.2 m.
Minimum Spacing: 1 m.
Propagation: Semi-hardwood cuttings.
Comments: Grows in a wide range of climates. Makes a good screen even if not clipped.

Macadamia integrifolia (Macadamia Nut)
M. tetraphylla
Height: 5 m.
Minimum Spacing: 2 m.
Propagation: Seed (soak in water for 24 hours before sowing). Good fruiting stock can be grafted onto seedling rootstock in late winter.
Comments: Frost-free districts.

Olea europaea (Fruiting Olive)
Height: 5 m.
Cut to: 2 m.
Minimum Spacing: 2 m.
Propagation: Seed. Semi-hardwood cuttings.
Comments: Slow growing. Must have full sun and good drainage.

Psidium littorale (Cherry Guava)
Height: 3 m.
Cut to: 1 m.
Minimum Spacing: 1 m.
Propagation: Seed.
Comments: Good screen with handsome, shiny leaves. Will take light frosts.

Hedges and Screens for Damp Spots
Alnus jorullensis (Evergreen Alder)
Height: 10 m.
Minimum Spacing: 3 m.
Propagation: Hardwood cuttings taken in late winter.
Comments: Fast growing, semi-evergreen in cooler climates. Needs ample water.

Casuarina glauca (**Swamp Oak**)
See Windbreaks p. 77.

Melaleuca quinquenervia (**Swamp Melaleuca**)
Height: 10 m.
Minimum Spacing: 3 m.
Propagation: Seed (seed capsules must be collected and allowed to dry).
Semi-hardwood cuttings.
Comments: Fast growing. Will survive in swamp conditions but can only
tolerate light frosts.

Salix chilensis '**Fastigiata**' (**Pencil Willow**)
Height: 8 m.
Minimum Spacing: 1 m.
Propagation: Hardwood cuttings in winter.
Comments: Must have ample water to look at its best. Will tolerate
moderate frosts but loses leaves in cold weather.

The Tall and Skinnies

Sometimes gardens have corridor-like sections where screening plants have to fit into a narrow area. These can occur along the sides of buildings or driveways and are very common between neighbours in suburban situations. The plants described in this section are of varying heights, but all have the characteristic of being much taller than they are wide.

One easy way of creating a screen in a narrow corridor is to erect a frame and cover it with a climbing plant. Most climbers are inclined to send out some horizontal shoots, however, which means that the screen will need regular clipping. It might be a better option to choose an upright growing shrub or tree from the limited range available. At one time bamboo would have been automatically planted in a narrow space and many uncontrollable acres have been covered as a result. Planting bamboo is no way to win friends and influence people, especially your neighbour, and may actually lead to legal proceedings — against you!

Nandina domestica, Japanese sacred bamboo, is an acceptable alternative to bamboo and spreads in a similar manner. This spread is much slower and more easily contained, however, and sacred bamboo has a lacy, delicate appearance. One of the main advantages of the plant is that it will grow in sun or shade, although sun is needed to bring out the red pigmentation of the leaves in winter. Sacred bamboo will grow to two metres and, if not confined, will gradually spread over a similar distance. It can lose some leaves and become thinner in the cooler months but even in the height of summer it is never more than a light screen.

Bamboo juniper (*Podocarpus macrophyllus* 'Maki') also accepts sun or shade and reaches about 2.5 metres. This dense, upright shrub makes a good wall plant with its squat, columnar habit that seldom exceeds one metre in width. It can be hard to find in nurseries but, if you can obtain some plants, it is worth growing for its formal, dark green, yew-like foliage. It's also useful for giving a Japanese air to a garden.

Our versatile friend, *Camellia sasanqua* grows in sun or shade and is easily persuaded into a narrow habit. Sasanquas are sometimes used as an espalier against a wall, which reduces the plant to a single horizontal plane, and the same sort of shaping can be achieved in a corridor. Choose some of the more upright growing varieties, such as 'Hiryu' (Kanjiro), 'Setsugekka', and 'Plantation Pink', and be prepared to trim them well after flowering. Three metres is a realistic height expectation, although they will grow larger in old age.

Most other upright growing plants need a fairly sunny situation, although *Pittosporum* 'James Stirling' is happy in half sun. It can get up to four metres and spread to two metres across, so may be a little wide for a very confined corridor. It can be a delightful fence plant with dainty foliage that picks well for flower arrangements.

Conifers are very popularly used as narrow screens and the Irish juniper (*Juniperus communis* 'Hibernica') makes a prickly, dark green column that gets to just over two metres. Like so many supposedly 'Irish' songs, this cultivar seems to have originated in the USA, but the dark green colour of the leaves should appeal to all true Irishmen, whether at home or abroad.

Irish juniper is slow growing and most gardeners would prefer to use a taller and faster conifer. The classic has always been the upright form of the Italian pencil pine (*Cupressus sempervirens* 'Stricta') which is seen, sentinel-like, surrounding so many Italian cemeteries. Unfortunately, it is often grown from seed and this leads to many genetic variations in shape. Some specimens have loose branches that hang wantonly out from the tree, spoiling the effect of the upright column. All that can be done in this case is to prune off the delinquent section or rein it in with some sort of tie. If choosing Italian pencil pines, try to obtain cutting-grown plants from a reliable source.

An Australian cultivar of the Italian pencil pine, 'Swane's Golden' was the first Australian-raised plant to receive a gold medal from the Australian Nurseryman's Association. It is a medium-rate grower which, unlike its Italian parent, tends to maintain a dense, compact, upright form. The foliage is a bright, yellow-gold but will revert to green if planted in too much shade. The tree can reach eight metres and is seldom more than one metre wide. It can be kept to a lesser height if clipping is commenced early in its life. Even when quite young it is often decorated with yellow, globular cones.

Both types of pencil pines need well-drained soil and good watering. Try to keep grass from growing over the tree's root area because grass roots are competitive and will rob the tree of nutrition. A layer of organic mulch is very important to protect the shallow conifer root system.

In warm climates the Bhutan cypress (*C. torulosa*) is narrow enough to qualify as a 'tall and skinny'. In frost-free areas it only spreads about one and a half metres but can cover about three times that in a cold district. Wall-like enclosures made up of Bhutan cypress are often seen as features in mountain gardens but the plant is versatile enough to grow anywhere short of the tropics if given a reliable supply of water.

We must return to Italy for another classic upright plant that has long been used to line fences and driveways. This is the Italian, or Lombardy, poplar (*Populus nigra* 'Italica') that grows rapidly and forms a pillar of golden colour in the autumn. It is not suitable for use in a suburban situation because its root system is too invasive and very inclined to sucker. In recent years poplar rust, a fungal disease, has become more and more of a menace and has reduced the tree's popularity. There is no practical way of treating this disease in large trees.

P. simonii 'Fastigiata' from China is often planted as a substitute for the Lombardy poplar and is much less inclined to sucker. It is smaller growing but, especially in humid areas, is still susceptible to poplar rust. Both these 'popular' poplars are deciduous and can be bought and transplanted at well-established heights in the dormant winter season.

Another deciduous tree that is rarely seen in Australian gardens is the upright form of the European hornbeam (*Carpinus betulus* 'Fastigiata'). 'Fastigiata' means 'upright' and this column-like tree is planted closely as a narrow screen in many famous European gardens. It grows naturally all over Europe and as far south as Persia so it is tolerant to a wide range of conditions; more so than the fastigiate beech (*Fagus sylvatica* 'Dawyck') which is also widely planted as a screen in Europe but is only used in moist, highland climates in Australia. The original Dawyck beech, found on the Dawyck estate in Scotland in 1860, is now about 90 metres tall but there is no danger of it approaching that height in the relatively shallow Australian soils. Although deciduous, both the beech and the hornbeam hang on to their dead leaves for most of the winter.

A relatively recent introduction to Australian gardens is the Chilean willow (*Salix chilensis* 'Fastigiata). This is also called the pencil willow for the obvious reason that it grows in a very upright, pencil-like shape. It is an excellent tree for a narrow position squeezed between a driveway and a fence and is tolerant to car exhaust fumes. It has very high water requirements and can grow with its roots in constantly soggy soil. Although these roots are not as invasive as those of the weeping willow (*S. babylonica*) they will go searching for water if left to fend for themselves in a dry garden bed.

Chilean willow is classed as an evergreen, but will become thinner during a cool winter. It grows to about eight metres and is 1.5 metres wide. Its growth is very upright and twiggy and is clothed in typical willow leaves. The whole effect of a well-grown plant is similar to that of a clump of healthy bamboo. Some plants have a better shape than others and I would advocate starting a friendship with someone who has some good specimens and begging them for some cuttings. Like most willows, the Chilean variety will sprout roots if cuttings are left in water for a few weeks. Winter hardwood cuttings can even be pushed directly into moist ground. Propagating your own plants could protect you from another frustrating problem — because the trees' water requirements are so high, nurserymen find them hard to maintain in good condition and they can often be difficult to find in nurseries.

The hop bush (*Dodonaea viscosa*) is a cosmopolitan shrub that occurs mostly in the southern hemisphere, but it is the New Zealand form with purple leaves that is most often used as a component in a narrow screen. *D. viscosa* 'Purpurea' was discovered on the banks of the Wairau River in the South Island in the 1930s and has been distributed all over the world since then. It grows upright to between two and three metres and is only about one metre wide. It has purplish bronze leaves and decorative red seed pods that last well into winter. It is fast-growing and, unfortunately, short-lived, but tends to last longer if regularly pruned. Watch out for stem borers and cut out affected sections when they are first noticed. The name 'hop bush' is variously described as being chosen because of the hop-like fruits or because the early settlers used the sticky fruit to make beer.

It's hard to find Australian natives that have a tall and skinny shape but you can count on anything with 'stricta' in its name as having such a profile. 'Stricta' is derived from the Latin word for stiff or straight and refers to the plant's upright growth. *Acacia stricta* grows wild in Victoria, New South Wales and Tasmania and is very fast and short-lived. It is best used by being mass planted in a narrow area, allowed to produce plenty of seed, and culled regularly to remove the older plants. This gives a rapid, upright screen about two metres high that would fit in well with an informal, native garden.

Checklist: The Tall and Skinnies

Acacia stricta (Upright Wattle)
Height: 3 m.
Minimum Spacing: 60 cm.
Propagation: Seed. Scarify by pouring boiling water on seeds and allow to cool before sowing.
Comments: Fast growing. Not the most attractive wattle but useful in a narrow area.

Camellia hiemalis 'Kanjiro' or 'Hiryu'
C. sasanqua 'Setsugekka'
C. sasanqua 'Plantation Pink'
See Medium Hedges and Screens p. 53.

Carpinus betulus 'Fastigiata' (European Hornbeam)
Height: 8 m.
Minimum Spacing: 1.2 m.
Propagation: Grafted onto seedling rootstock.
Comments: Best in cool, mountain climates. Deciduous, but holds some leaves during winter.

Cupressus sempervirens 'Stricta' (Italian Pencil Pine)
Height: 8 m.
Minimum Spacing: 1 m.
Propagation: Seed (there will be some seedling variation). Semi-hardwood cuttings.
Comments: Needs good sun and good drainage but will grow in a wide range of climates.

C. sempervirens 'Swanes Golden' (Swanes Golden Pencil Pine)
Height: 8 m.
Minimum Spacing: 60 cm.
Propagation: Semi-hardwood cuttings.
Comments: Very narrow, medium grower for a wide range of climates. Must have full sun and good drainage.

C. torulosa (Bhutan Cypress)
See Medium Hedges and Screens p. 55.

Dodonaea viscosa 'Purpurea' (Purple Hop Bush)

Height: 3 m.
Minimum Spacing: 60 cm.
Propagation: Seed.
Comments: Fast growing and shortlived. Needs a sunny position.

Fagus sylvatica 'Dawyck' (Upright Beech)
Height: 8 m.
Minimum Spacing: 1.2 m.
Propagation: Grafted onto seedling rootstock.
Comments: Best in cool, mountain climates. Deciduous, but hangs onto most of its leaves through winter.

Juniperus communis 'Hibernica' (Irish Juniper)
Height: 2 m.
Minimum Spacing: 75 cm.
Propagation: Semi-hardwood cuttings.
Comments: Slow growing. Must have full sun and good drainage. Cold hardy.

Nandina domestica (Japanese Sacred Bamboo)
See Low Hedges and Screens p. 40.

Pittosporum tenuifolium 'James Stirling' (James Stirling Pittosporum)
See Tall Screens p. 69.

Podocarpus macrophyllus 'Maki' (Bamboo Juniper)
Height: 2 m.
Minimum Spacing: 60 cm.
Propagation: Semi-hardwood cuttings (difficult).
Comments: Dark green, bamboo-like foliage. Will grow in sun or shade and tolerate cold conditions.

Populus nigra 'Italica' (Lombardy Poplar)
P. simonii 'Fastigiata' (Simon's Poplar)
Height: 8–10 m.
Minimum Spacing: 2 m.
Propagation: Hardwood cuttings in winter.
Comments: Deciduous trees that grow well in cooler areas. Lombardy poplar is inclined to sucker.

Salix chilensis 'Fastigiata' (Pencil Willow)
See Special Purpose Hedges and Screens p. 98.

Problem Plants

Hedges were very fashionable in the 19th century and Australian gardeners experimented with many plants that were suitable for hedging but were hardy enough to survive the rigours of the Australian climate. Unfortunately, some of these introductions performed so successfully in our climate that they went on to become weeds and are now competing with the native bush plants.

The classic example is the small-leafed privet from China (*Ligustrum sinense*) which makes an almost perfect hedge. It has close, small growth that responds well to shearing and it will grow in sun or shade. It seems able to survive in coastal areas without supplementary watering and continues to thrive even when its roots are periodically inundated with water. It grows readily from seed and this is its downfall; the summer berries are attractive to birds and they spread the seeds far and wide.

There is a closely related species, large-leafed privet (*L. lucidum*), and both types produce an abundance of spring flowers. These are small, creamy-white and have a heavy scent that is known to cause hayfever. After flowering, clumps of blue-black fruit form and each small tree is capable of producing thousands of berries. When these seeds germinate in bushland they can create impenetrable thickets that block the light from native plants in the immediate vicinity. Eventually, lack of light kills the native plants and the heavy cover prevents the germination of replacement seedlings. Within a few years, a patch of bushland can become a monoculture of privet.

To their credit, nurserymen are no longer propagating privet plants but if you have inherited a privet hedge the only responsible way of maintaining it is to cut off the dead flowers before the seed heads develop. There is a golden-leafed form of the large-leafed privet that is sometimes sold and, because it is sterile, it seems to be quite safe to use.

A distant relative of the privet, African olive (*Olea africana*), has also escaped from the fenceline and invaded the bush. While in no way constituting the menace that privet has become, African olive has some free-seeding tendencies that have spoilt its reputation. It is a very hardy

shrub with long, yellow-green leaves and bird-attracting black fruit that
are only a fraction of the size of edible olives. It is still sometimes seen
in nurseries but is best avoided if you live anywhere near bushland.

All of these plants can be destroyed by cutting the trunk near ground
level and immediately painting the cut stump with a strong solution
of glyphosate. You can use a similar method to get rid of another pest,
Mickey Mouse plant (*Ochna serrulata*). This is such an innocent looking
shrub with cheerful, yellow flowers and black berries backed by a bright
red calyx, that it is hard to believe it could ever cause trouble. Once
it seeds in the bush, however, it immediately sends down a long tap
root that gives it a very firm hold on the ground. It is still occasionally
seen as a formally clipped hedge.

Many of our screening pests were introduced by homesick
Englishmen who wanted to recreate the hedgerows of their distant
homeland. European plants such as the briar rose (*Rosa rubiginosa*), gorse
(*Ulex europeus*), and some of the brooms spread to invade recently cleared
pastures and broke many a farmer's heart. Shrubs from other parts
of the world were also employed to form hedgerows and were tough
enough to survive in the Australian countryside. They included berrying
plants like the Chinese firethorns (*Pyracantha* species), the American
and European hawthorns, and the Chinese cotoneasters. All of these
have brightly coloured fruit and are easily spread by birds.

African boxthorn (*Lycium ferocissimum*), another hedgerow shrub, is
armed with fierce spines which help protect it from eradication attempts.
It can be found growing wild all over Australia and is a declared noxious
weed in the south-eastern states. It has pretty white or mauve flowers
and attractive scarlet berries. Its thickets of spiny growth are perfect
for harbouring rabbits.

In a similar manner, blackberries (*Rubus fruticosus*) were planted as
dividers along boundaries and have spread all over the countryside where
they are particularly troublesome in cool, moist areas. Blackberry is
a declared noxious weed in all states and comes in a number of slightly
different forms. It can spread by means of underground rhizome-like
roots, by seed from the tasty fruit, and by layering when the long,
arching canes touch the ground. Like the African boxthorn, blackberries
make a wonderful hiding place for rabbits. Blackberries are notoriously
difficult to eradicate and persistent digging or poisoning seems to be
the only way to win the blackberry war.

Tree lucerne (*Chamaecytisus proliferus*), another hedgerow plant, is a native of the Canary Islands (the Canary Islands must be a very tough place — so many of its plants seem to be virtually indestructible!). Tree lucerne is currently in fashion as a quick growing fodder plant and, like all legumes, can convert atmospheric nitrogen to a useable form. It has spread and caused problems in Victoria, Tasmania and South Australia.

Some plants that were originally employed as part of a seaside shelter belt have gone on to become full-blown weeds. One of the most invasive is the South African daisy which is called boneseed (*Chrysanthemum monilifera*). This three metre tall shrub has bright yellow flowers and a hard, bone-like seed. It looks deceptively cheerful as it flowers in the full teeth of the coastal winds, but it is just waiting for a chance to spread to nearby bushland.

Italian lavender (*Lavandula stoechas*) can also be used as a low growing component in a coastal screen. This popular garden shrub has become a serious pasture pest in Victoria and South Australia. Even in coastal districts it is capable of spreading but it only becomes a nuisance on open, badly disturbed sites. It is grown for its dark coloured flowers which are very attractive to bees.

One of the major pest plants in NSW and Queensland is lantana (*Lantana camara*). It was often used as a quick-growing hedge in frost-free climates and has been readily spread by the birds that eat the black fruit. Its blooms are made up of clusters of tubular flowers that usually have cream and pink colouring, although there is a form with red flower clusters. Lantana is one of the worst weeds of the east coast and is seen forming dense thickets in the open, or scrambling up trees in the bush. Its shallow root system is easily removed by hand, but working amongst the rasp-like stems can be a dangerous occupation.

The screening plant that must cause the greatest number of problems between neighbours is bamboo. Bamboo is one of the world's most important economic plants and is really just an overgrown grass, but try telling that to someone who has it invading from next door. It is very difficult to contain and, for that reason, is seldom planted. It can be killed by using glyphosate, but this is a tedious job.

There are two main genera: *Bambusa* and *Phyllostachys*. *Bambusa* is called 'clumping' bamboo and spreads more slowly than the *Phyllostachys* species that snakes outwards with lateral rhizomes. Unfortunately, they are often badly labelled in nurseries and the easiest way to tell the difference between the two types is to look at the vein pattern on the leaves. *Phyllostachys* veins have a network pattern while *Bambusa* veins run parallel to each other. Either way, don't plant bamboo unless you can contain it with a metre-deep barrier or, better still, keep it confined to a pot.

References

Bay Books, *Encyclopaedia of Australian Gardening*. Bay Books, Sydney, 1978.

Hall, E & T , *Trees and Shrubs For Australian Gardens*. Pan, Sydney, 1980.

Lord, E.E. & Willis J.H., *Shrubs and Trees For Australian Gardens*. 5th Edition, Lothian, Melbourne, 1982.

Nicholson, N. & H., *Rainforest Plants 3*. Terania Rainforest Nursery, The Channon, 1991.

Palmer, S.J., *Palmer's Manual of Trees, Shrubs and Climbers*. Palmer's Garden Centre, Auckland, NZ.

Plumridge, J., *How To Propagate Plants*. Lothian, Melbourne, 1983.

Rowell, R.J., *Ornamental Flowering Shrubs In Australia*. Reed, Sydney, 1980.

Rowell, R.J., *Ornamental Flowering Trees In Australia*. Reed, Sydney, 1980.

Readers Digest, *Your Gardening Questions Answered*. Readers Digest, Sydney, 1989.

Swane, V., *Gregory's Australian Gardening Guide*. Gregory's, Sydney, 1985.

Wrigley, J.W. & Fagg M., *Australian Native Plants*. 2nd Edition, Collins, Sydney, 1983.

Index